Praise for Br

"This brave book feels like a healthier version of the game truth or dare, one in which we dare to be true to ourselves. We can shed the shame and blame to heal core wounds and lean into pure joy. The empowering examples and exercises help us to strengthen our own inner warrior, who holds the keys to set our brave heart free so we can thrive from the inside out. Through these pages, I feel the courage and confidence to live uncensored and uncaged!" ~ **Julia Ostara,** Artist, Explorer, Creator of 2 oracle card decks, & Author of *The Girl Who Dances With Delight*

"Loved this book. This is an inspiring book for every wounded healer, who knows they need to share their story, their truth, their insight or nuggets of wisdom. Laura's rawness, her tremendous courage and braveness is deeply inspiring and yet healing. It certainly has motivated and helped me to start writing on a completely different level." ~ **Eileen Burns,** Owner of Stress Coach Training

"If you are aware that you have greatness within you and are ready to heal the wounds that have held you back; if you are ready to move towards the greatness you know you're meant to live, this book is for you. Laura Di Franco's life experience and exceptional tools can powerfully assist your journey in accessing the inner warrior goddess that is waiting to emerge." ~**Veronica B. Light**, Spiritual Mentor and Author

"If anyone desires significant alterations to the life they're currently living – whether they are merely thinking about what they want to do, or they are truly ready to effect life changes – then this book is perfect for them. Laura says it herself: she "gets you". She knows where you are and what you are looking at, and she is here offering a hand and a direction for movement, so the reader can accomplish whatever new life they desire." ~ **Karen Fulkerson,** Kick ass, take names. No regrets.

I wanted to return all my other books about healing to the shelf and just practice these teachings. The book offers nothing-to-hide tools, compassionate and wise. ~**Manuela Rohr,** Yoga Teacher and Phoenix Rising Yoga Therapist, C-IAYT

Brave Healing

A Guide for Your Journey

Laura Di Franco, MPT

ISBN: 978-1-947486-05-8

Published and distributed by Possibilities Publishing Company
PossibilitiesPublishingCompany.com
Burke, VA

Some names in this book have been changed
to minimize my stress levels after this is published.

My Street Cred:

Just who do I think I am to write this book? Maybe you want to know why you should read it. Or listen to me. Or how I found the courage?

A lifelong sparring match with unworthiness work for you? That's not enough, is it? You want to feel my pain. Know how I survived. You gotta be able to say, "Me too!" And you gotta trust me.

I feel you.

I hope my vulnerable, courageous stories will inspire you. That you'll think, "Holy shit, she's brave." And you'll start to be brave too. I hope you'll start living the life you crave, today. I hope the tools I've practiced and offer in this book inspire you to take action on living your amazing life.

I've made a life and career out of healing. Rather than boring you with any of my bio here, let me just say that after over two decades studying what healing means, I feel a commitment and duty to offer up what I know to help you on your way. My wish is that this book inspires you to wonder what else is possible, and then go after it more intensely than you ever have before; unapologetically and wildly exploring the terrain of your body, mind and soul and then performing the most magnificent cannon ball straight into your most fiercely alive life and self.

But if it helps, just know I've dedicated myself to understanding healing in several ways. Through being a holistic physical therapist, a published author and a third degree black belt in Tae Kwon Do, I've studied how to feel my best physically, mentally and spiritually. I've taught others these tools for years. What I know is that there might just be something you haven't learned yet that could change everything!

Let's start this journey!

Table of Contents

Foreword

by John F. Barnes, PT
founder of JFB Myofascial Release

I've had the opportunity and privilege of knowing Laura for a long period of time now. She is a very highly skilled Myofascial Release therapist, a black belt in tae kwon do, has a multitude of talents, including being an incredible writer.

One of the things I ask in my Myofascial Release seminars is 'What is your mission? What is the purpose of your life?' You might want to consider asking yourself those questions, quieting down, but no need for an answer right away, as it might take a little time. I'll explain in a few moments. Most of us live our life without really understanding our unique mission in this lifetime, so much time and effort is squandered. It's like a team of horses going in opposite directions, like we're being pulled apart and distracted constantly. It weakens us versus when you learn to have focus and be centered in what I call Channel 3, it's like the team of horses now going in the same direction and it's a very powerful experience. All of your decisions should be made in alignment with your particular mission.

I've been treating people from all over the world with Myofascial Release for over 50 years now. A simplistic way of looking at consciousness is what I call Channel 5 and Channel 3. Channel 5 is our intellectual, rational, linear side, while Channel 3 is our intuitive, instinctive side which I consider to be the healing zone. It's the creative side of Channel 3 that good writers learn to tap into. This is also another way to describe our feeling intelligence. See and feel the words you are writing and the story you are attempting to convey. Another word for that is wisdom.

We're all are born with amazing wisdom, but our education system, which is more mass hypnosis than true education, kind of beat it out of us. You've all heard the quote, "If you don't define yourself, somebody else will." and that's what happened to most of us. We're a product more of other people's thoughts and programming.

Neuroscientists have discovered that the database available to us in Channel 3 is in excess of 10 million to 1 of that of our intellectual side. The whole focus of our society and healthcare has been Channel 5, that miniscule level of consciousness. I believe that Channel 3 is what I have heard Laura call our 'authentic self.' It isn't until we discover our authentic self by our inner work, Myofascial Release, writing, and other forms of therapy do we truly become fully alive and learn to be healthy and enjoy our life! Channel 5 is about fear, criticism, negativity, and judgement, while Channel 3 is about love, clarity and compassion. What path do you choose?

Thank You!

In a book that was manifested from the magical power of gratitude, I'm at a loss for just the perfect words to express just how much I feel right now. It's ginormous and overwhelming. It's so good.

I couldn't have made this book happen without the fierce, unconditional and steadfast love of Susan, Shelly, Phil or Chris. You each have a deed to large parts of my heart.

This book is dedicated to all the warrior souls journeying alongside me on the path: the students, teachers, fellow healers and writers, the BFF, the friends, family, lovers, ex-lovers and children, the online friends and the random acquaintances. And Mom; I love you.

Thank you for the awareness, the lessons, the insights, ahas, the love and the miracles. Thanks for the way you show me the light, and the way you love me through the darkness. Thank you for helping me know myself. May we all enjoy this journey and thrive!

Meredith, thank you so much for believing in me and taking this project on as your baby too!

Special thanks to Stacey Littledeer for the amazing front-cover artwork. You can find her at SpiritFireArt.com

A huge thank you to Tammi Nolan Metzler of TheWriteAssociate.com for taking special editing care of my baby.

Thank you to The Writer's Center for accepting that first pitch for the Writing as a Path to Healing workshop and supporting me with everything that's happened since!

For everyone who cheers me on, supports my work and refers their friends, thanks for trusting and believing in me. To my badass book launch team: you guys are phenomenal! Throughout this entire process I felt showered with love and because of that feeling I knew this was meant to be.

To my readers and clients: the purpose with which I'm filled every day since this work started pouring through me is like nothing I've ever experienced, and that is because you continue to tell me how your lives have been changed by it. I write to heal, so that I can give that energy back to you. And so that you can take it and run like wildfire, with a new courage and energy of your own. What an amazing thing to feel what you were born for and to feel part of a ripple.

Introduction

The Dealbreaker

"Let's all go around and say what we're grateful f—"

"No! We're not going to do that!" My husband interrupted my request, blasting me in front of our son and daughter at the Thanksgiving table that night. The spear pierced my heart and I bit my tongue, choking back the blood and tears that threatened to overflow. Rather than speaking, I devoured the meal I'd just spent hours preparing and serving by myself as quickly as possible and excused myself to the bedroom of our new log home in the woods. The home we'd dreamed about for years that I'd woken up in feeling so grateful for on our first holiday there together.

Instead of sharing that appreciation with those closest to me, I lay devastated on top of the covers of my bed in the dark staring out the window at the moon, tears falling freely down my face. I could hear the silence on the other side of the door where the rest of my family sat eating their meal without me. *What the fuck?* I thought. *It's fucking Thanksgiving. The one holiday devoted to gratitude. And he can't even let me express myself? It's not like I've asked to say Grace. I'm not praising God right now. I'm expressing thanks.*

My mind was too full. I was nauseated by his lack of gratitude and generosity and that feeling infected my gut and my thoughts. Everything I should have done and said was crashing in on me. Why couldn't I stand back up, walk out there and say, "I'm going to say what I'm grateful for, and if you don't feel like listening or participating then you might want to leave the room for a few minutes." Or something like, "Fuck you asshole, it's Thanks-fucking-giving, and I just made this whole meal solo. And we're fucking sitting in our new, second home in the woods. What the fuck is wrong with you?"

That would have felt better. Or possibly the latter part with a bit of compassion could have worked. But instead I sat in my room for the rest of the night. I did not have permission to be angry. I could not speak up. I felt suffocated for the thousandth time in my life and our marriage and was beginning to wonder how many more times I could feel that way and not want to die.

It was the first time I knew I couldn't stay with someone who lacked a certain level of generosity. *What am I going to do?* I cried to myself. I pulled the white down comforter up over my shoulders, turned my back to the door and hoped I'd pass out before he joined me in bed.

The stories I'll share in this tool-book might shock you. How can she write about that stuff? You might wonder. How's she so brave? Isn't she afraid of what other people will think?

I am. Afraid, that is. But I've learned to be afraid and do it anyway. I've learned, through more than two decades devoted to a powerful holistic healing practice, that the only way through is to feel everything and then do what you're afraid to do. I've come to know my worth. And now it's time for you to know yours.

A Breakthrough

"Do you like key lime pie?" Dr. Jeff Smith, an East Coast radiologist, took it upon himself to make sure I tasted the concoction made from Delta airline's Biscoff cookies and lime juice. Flight 1101 was taking us back from Whitefish to Baltimore that afternoon in February of 2015, a few days shy of my 47th birthday.

"The flight attendant on my last trip told me about this," he said, now with the attention of our flight attendant, who was surprisingly interested in what my seatmate had to say. Stopping her cart for several minutes to listen—and blocking up the aisle in the process—she provided us with said ingredients.

We also had the attention of her cart partner, who was so excited about our request that he found two fresh bananas in some secret part of the cart and insisted we put a small piece in between our lime-soaked cookies.

I knew the minute I sat down in seat 11C that I wasn't going to be able to carry out my personal flight plan. Dr. Smith had extended his hand before my butt hit the seat, making me hurry to get my juggling act under control and introduce myself. Full contemplation, reflection and note copying from my four days in the heaven of my first writing retreat in Montana would have to wait; I had some key lime pie to make.

"Here, look at this," Dr. Smith said just moments later, literally shoving his laptop onto the leftover corner of my tiny tray table, already occupied by my own laptop. "My kids went here, it's a camp in Canada. See if you can find the pictures or a video to look at." He eagerly watched as I began to scroll down the homepage of Camp BillBob, or Billbo, or Billwood, or something like that. *This keyboard must be fairly clean*, I thought, *him being a doctor and all.*

By the end of the flight I knew he was coming home from a ski trip in Bozeman. He and his wife had just attended the wedding of their daughter in Florida, and she was one of two daughters, both of which had spent whole summers at Camp BillBob. I knew his wife was still in Florida, and he did not have to return to work at the hospital tomorrow, so he was less stressed than usual.

I also discovered that one of his daughters was an occupational therapist and that he and his wife like her fiancé. "You know that will be the kiss of death, that we actually like this guy," he said.

This feels so good, I thought to myself. *For once talking to strangers feels good.* I smiled as I listened to him talk about his life, watching his face and allowing him to see mine.

"How do you like it?" Dr. Smith was genuinely interested in my answer about the cookie concoction.

"This's the best airline cookie key lime pie I've ever tasted," I replied. I turned my head toward him easily and lingered there, letting him see the smile in my eyes. I took a deep breath and emailed the BillBob camp from his computer to ask for information, even though I'd just explained to him our summer was already booked.

"It's a really great camp," he said for the seventh time. I believed him.

Transitioning from Fear to Love

If the eyes are the window to the soul, get out your Windex, people. Rub the panes clean until the light shines through. By cleaning off the layers of dirt covering my soul, I can see and feel love for a perfect stranger, for my ex-husband, my client in chronic pain, my dog, the cow on the side of the road, the tree in my backyard, my mom, (who can't stand when I use the word fuck in my writing), and for my dad, who once admitted his love for me was conditional.

I'm at a point in my life now that I love talking with people and learning about what makes them tick. I didn't use to. I used to be so painfully shy that being in a room full of people would cause chest pain. My self-esteem was so low I couldn't talk to anyone. Looking them in the eye was impossible.

I lived my life in fear. Fear of what others thought of me, fear of doing things the wrong way, fear of failing, speaking up, being myself and claiming my power and purpose in the world. I hid behind the label of introvert for years, holding back my real, wild, sexy, badass, enthusiastic self until she was sick and exhausted.

Today, I feel so much different. Past wounds have become opportunities for brave healing. Current-day triggers have become opportunities for deep awareness and transformation. I look at the world with curiosity now. I believe in the magic of positive thinking, vibration and manifestation. I feel fiercely alive and am enjoying my moments more than I ever have. I'm attracting some big love and abundance into my life.

My healing came in layers and stages, some more stuck and crusty than others. Those layers of past pain and disappointment peeled off with each word I wrote in my journal, each self-growth workshop I took, each new Tae Kwon Do kick I learned, and each aware moment I spent with my acupuncturist, breathworker, bodyworker, psychotherapist, Emotional

Freedom Technique (EFT) practitioner and John F. Barnes Myofascial Release colleagues.

My life and career have been about exploring awareness and healing, in all forms. No matter who I was with or what I was doing, healing came because I woke up and started to be brave. Awareness, self-love and courage helped me ditch the label of introvert (as a shield) and heal the pain and fear that kept me from playing big in the world.

Recently, healing came furiously in a room of ten women who shared a common longing for expressing their awesomeness with words on the page. That energy and love lingers in my heart now as I sit on the plane pondering how I'll achieve reentry into a life that now feels more alien than before.

It's taken me a couple of decades and a career in healing to re-discover the self-worth I lost as a child, transform that pain and step into my passion and power. I'm a warrior goddess. You might recognize your own story here in mine, so let's get to the important business of healing your shit, so you don't have to spend one more day letting your pain paralyze you or only wishing for a life you love. It's my turn to help you be brave and do the healing work that'll change everything.

And in case you need more proof than what's above, here's my actual bio:

I'm an expert holistic physical therapist, John F. Barnes Myofascial Release and CranioSacral Therapy practitioner, a published author of a memoir and four poetry journals, and a third-degree black belt in Tae Kwon Do.

My writing is all over the internet in places like *The Huffington Post*, *MindBodyGreen*, *The Elephant Journal*, *Tiny Buddha* and *Glamour.com*. My *Writing as a Path to Healing and Intuitive Writing for Healers* workshops are changing the way people think about how they heal.

And just for fun, you might be interested to know that my hobbies include raving, drag racing, writing love poems and walking in the woods. If you bring me dark chocolate we'll be friends forever. If you sit down with me to talk about sex, death, the stars, and/or why we're here on this earth, you'll have my undivided attention.

Some things I know for sure: My kids (and yours) are a miracle and will change the world. Animals are healers too. The Universe speaks in rainbows, and eagles and the way the light moves through the glass block window and settles in recognizable shapes on the wall. And if you're paying attention long enough to learn her language, you can have and be anything you want to have or be.

I've strived my whole life to understand and share my unique process of healing with others and to guide them on this sometimes impossible journey. I've spent hundreds of hours journaling, lying on the table, sitting in the therapy chair and sharing my vulnerable stories, publishing some of them. I've spent over eleven years kicking through my fear in the dojang. I've explored, doubted and rediscovered—over and over again—what it means to heal, in an attempt to help others in some small way.

Brave healing is a lifestyle for which you need certain important tools. This book was meant to help you break the habits keeping you unhappy and unhealthy by teaching you the healing practice of feeling. The tool of body awareness is something you'll practice your whole life and it'll start to change things in big ways.

The tool of mastering your mindset will bring you to the next level of awareness you'll need: watching and feeling the thoughts sabotaging and paralyzing you, then creating new ones to better serve your joy and health. The tool of thought awareness is something you'll practice forever, if you're interested in living bravely and fiercely alive.

The tool of daily courage will help you integrate the body and mind with the action steps you'll need to take to be brave every single day. This will be another important tool in your kit—your Bravery Toolkit—and will keep you on track and unapologetically aligned with the desires, dreams and goals burning inside you.

I'll share the gift of my knowledge, experience and my pain in the pages to follow. Join me on this journey. Be brave. It's worth it. It's time to thrive.

10 Tips for
Getting The Most
Out of This Book!

I get high on big questions. What's your next move? What do you love doing so much that you lose track of time? What are you really good at? What's something that would surprise us about you? What are you feeling right now? If there were nobody left to upset or disappoint, who would you become? And one of my all-time favorite quotes: "Tell me, what do you plan to do with your one wild and precious life?" Mary Oliver

I don't know, I think. This's harder than I thought. I don't know what I want, or who I am, or what to do, or how I feel. *What if you did know?* I hear.

Those words shoot through to my soul. The core part of me that knows is slapped awake and I realize all the shit I'm piling in the way of my happiness and healing. I can't speak.

Truth is I'm afraid to say how I feel, what I want, who I am, and what I love. I'm afraid to be me. It's not that I don't know who I am, it's that I'm afraid you won't like her.

The Healing

My composure cracks open and tears fall for minutes, seemingly hours. I can't stop them.

"You can do this," my partner at the Myofascial Release class grounds herself and holds a healing space, making it safe to be vulnerable. "It's okay to feel this," she continues as I lie on the portable, purple massage table surrounded by fifty others, in a dimly-lit ballroom at the Holiday Inn.

This's hard. Nobody in physical therapy school taught me about this kind of healing. Nobody told me I'd have to be a warrior for my own health, joy and life. They just told me to memorize body parts. I was good at that, at getting A's; following rules; obeying my parents, teachers and coaches; and being a perfect, good girl. I was also painfully shy and totally unconscious; unable to feel.

Forty-year-old tears flow at last through the choking knot in my throat, working their way to the surface. I'd rather be anywhere else, be doing anything other than touching these raw places inside of me. "Stay with it," my partner says. I do, until the tears dry up and something clicks. I get a glimpse of my essence: pure love and joy. *I'm enough,* I think. *I'm worthy. I can do anything I want to do,* the voice in my head says.

It'd been so long since I heard a voice like that. I felt a shift in that moment. Something good was coming.

The places this healing work has taken me are a quantum leap toward freedom, health and pure joy. The process sucks sometimes and feels impossible some days, but I can count on movement toward my wildest desires if I persevere. This healing journey requires a warrior. But not the kind I learned about in school.

I've been asked several times why I use the word "warrior." Many people think of war, fighting, or violence when they hear that word. I use it differently. A warrior soul possesses the indomitable spirit required to live with disciplined, fierce awareness in the moment-to-moment stuff of their life.

They show up for all of it and use awareness to align with what serves their bigger goals, dreams and purpose. They're then able to change the way they think, believe and act so they're responding instead of reacting to their moments. They're able to transform their fear to courage and their pain to freedom and create a life they love and that changes the world.

Being a warrior on your healing journey means you voluntarily show up and step into the arena, whether or not you think you'll get your ass kicked, and be your vulnerable self. The warrior is connected with an inner guide and has learned his/her language. This kind of warrior won't settle for a "meh" life. This kind of healing takes courage. This kind of person recognizes a soul-level pull toward their desire to play bigger, for the purpose of moving toward joy and inspiring others to do the same.

Brave healing is an unapologetic journey to joy. It's about truly thriving.

Healing used to mean recovering from an injury, wound or surgery. It wasn't very messy, complicated or integrated. It was black and white. Good or bad. Right or wrong. A cookbook to follow. The right way didn't include room for feelings, emotions, dreams, magic or bliss. It meant you followed certain rules, should's and supposed to's. There were protocols to memorize. Serendipity? What's that?

The definition of healing I understand after over twenty years in the field, working to help thousands of people heal, is way different, way more holistic, and much more rewarding than I could've ever imagined. What healing means to me now is the difference between a life I'm tolerating and a life that turns me on. It's the difference between content and blissed out. Between just functioning and peak performance.

I wrote this book to help you redefine healing so you can make your own rules and experience everything you know there is to experience in the life you crave.

I'm called to teach this warrior kind of healing and invite you to come on the journey with me. Ready to discover your inner warrior? I'll be your guide today.

What if there are things you haven't learned yet that could change everything?

I'm going to share the powerful tools I've learned about healing with you. This's an invitation to dive deeper and explore the undiscovered territory of your soul's desires. Grab my hand and join me on this epic journey of Brave Healing. I'll tell you all the secrets I've learned and everything I know about how to be brave and thrive in your life.

Even better, grab a friend and do this book with them. Find a community that lifts you up, that you can have this kind of bigger conversation with, full of people who love to get high on big questions. Move through this book together. Accountability will be one of the magical keys to taking action and following through.

10 tips for getting every juicy morsel out of this book:

1. **Do the exercises.** Reading through and skimming over the exercises the first time is cool, but nothing happens without action. Doing the exercises is going to help you move closer to what you desire. Let the ideas in this book light a fire under your ass and take action!

2. **Get together with someone you trust**, someone you can have "that kind" of conversation with, and do the exercise and/or discuss the Warrior Questions at the end of each chapter together. You'll gain powerful insights and accelerate your learning and growing by collaborating with other warriors. This won't be just a book club; you'll create a Brave Healing Community.

3. **Keep a special notebook handy** for the exercises and to write down your takeaways. Your notebook's going to be a valuable resource later on and can serve as a blueprint for action and your goals. Have it with you when you pick up this book to read.

4. **Share your dreams**, insights and ahas in the Brave Healers Mastermind and Refuge Facebook group. Connect with other warriors for inspiration, ideas and motivation. When you're brave and can move the ideas in your head to the outside world by speaking up, they become real. Consider finding an accountability partner to work with you on your goals.

5. **Get some help**. Everyone needs some therapy and/or coaching when it comes to healing and living their kick-ass life. Find someone you vibe with and invest in yourself. Having a coach or therapist in your corner pushing you to be your magnificent self is priceless. They'll see stuff you can't. If you can't afford a coach, then get on your favorite websites and devour any free information you can get your hands on, talk to others who're doing what you want to be doing. Ask a lot of questions. You don't have to do this alone.

6. **Be afraid, and do it anyway.** When you bump up against something I've written and you feel resistance, stop and feel. This's the nugget, the opportunity, the exact piece that can catapult you to another level of evolution, if you're willing to go there. Be brave.

7. **Be willing to examine everything**—and I do mean everything, good, bad, and indifferent— that happens to you as if it were an opportunity in disguise. Be open, curious, and playful about your life. Begin to use your intuition and inner warrior to guide you. Learn how to trust it. Practice, practice, practice. If something bugs, annoys, angers or frustrates you, pay attention. Look at what you resist.

8. **The key to everything is awareness.** Without it, you won't have any choice but to feel like you are a victim of circumstance. Pay particular attention to chapter one. Read it a couple times if you have to. It will be the foundation for the rest of the book, and the rest of your amazing life. When in doubt, wake up. Look in and observe your thoughts and feelings.

9. **Start a practice of body awareness**, breathing or meditation while you're moving through the lessons in this book. You'll find a simple exercise in the first chapter to get you started and more resources at the end of the book.

10. **Stay awake!** When you hear the voice in your head saying that you aren't enough or what you're doing isn't good, right or worthy, or if you begin to doubt everything, lose hope or become depressed and fearful, hear this: it's all bullshit. Your very thoughts are what're getting in the way of the love, joy, magic, miracles, healing and bliss you desire. Shut it down and choose a better, more healthy way to think, believe and act…a way that serves your bigger purpose. Be brave!

Now, let's get to some thriving lessons!

Start right here, right now, by dropping down deep into your feeling senses. Feel the book you're holding: notice its crisp pages, inhale the smell of new ink. Feel your body on the chair, the clothes on your body. Notice what's going through your mind. Clear the chatter and connect with your breath.

I want you to experience this book, not just read it. I want you to allow your body to walk through these pages, by noticing what you feel as you read. Notice yourself checking out? Stop. Take a pause. Connect with the breath again and then check back in.

You'll notice through some passages you might be tensing, even holding your breath. Challenge yourself to stay present, be curious about what you feel, and continue to stay connected to the feeling senses, aware as you move through the words. Don't worry about doing this perfectly; it's a practice. And you can start right now. Noticing your resistance; what your body does when it feels triggered or threatened, is one of the keys to healing. When you're aware you have choices!

Deep breath. Let's do this.

1
Are You Asleep?

Take Me Higher
by Laura Di Franco

This dampness
sticks to my ribs
shrivels my breath
to a tiny wheeze.

I'm crippled
by the tight
shrink-wrap
around my heart.

The ache
becomes unbearable
and I cry
for help.

I can't seem
to find the answers
nothing's right
nothing's good.

All that's left
is to ache
hope
for a shift.

To feel
the parts

too frightening
to feel.

To go there
let go there
pray
and lay back in it.

Breathe into it.
Be in it.
Trust it

~~

Sitting in the four-bedroom brick, ranch-style home we bought just before my son was born, the voice in my head says, *It won't get any better than this. Just be happy with what you have. You don't need anything. You're healthy, your family's healthy.* It reminds me, wanting more is greedy. The "meh" feeling has become normal. It's easier to follow the rules and do what I'm supposed to do. And I'm supposed to be happy.

Resigned and content in a neutral sort of way, the lacking joy doesn't feel urgent. There're so many others with less. *Wanting more means being ungrateful,* I hear the voice say. *Getting too excited about anything's a set-up for disappointment. Expectations are bad.* My thoughts and beliefs have a voice in my head, and it's starting to feel suffocating.

I'm starting to recognize the voices as old, conditioned beliefs from my past, things I was taught to believe. From my mom. My dad. My first-grade teacher. My exercise physiology professor. My soccer coach. They all had a say. Everyone had a say but me.

Life duties and roles consume me. *Who you are is what you do and you do a lot, so you must be important,* the voice convinces. And being important is the goal. Achievement and success are the path to happiness. They quickly become my drug of choice.

The daily ache in my chest reeks of low-level resentment, poisoning my moments. It's getting worse. Anxiety feels normal. Life feels really short. *Something's missing,* whispers my desire voice. *Don't ignore me,* it says, pinging my chest with a familiar ache again. The yearning hurts now.

I know I need to make a change. My body's telling me to. *I wonder how much longer I can ignore it*, I say to myself.

By the time I'd accomplished everything on my list of to-do's, shoulds and supposed tos, I was sick and exhausted. Success wasn't bringing happiness like I thought it would. Being a college grad, a healer, a wife, a mom, a business owner and a marathon runner wasn't filling the aching hole in my soul.

I continued to try to fill the void by pursuing a black belt in Tae Kwon Do. Then my second degree black belt. And then my third. I thought being successful would make me happy.

I checked off each box dutifully, asleep to what I already should have been grateful for, unconscious about the choices I made and everyone involved in those choices. I made decisions based on other people's opinions of what was good, right and successful. I made decisions based on a desperate need to feel worthy and for others to like me.

When I flew across the country after grad school and moved into a one-bedroom studio with my boyfriend (now my ex) there were no promises of commitment. I was so infatuated with him that I sorted out my internship on the East Coast, packed up, and said goodbye to my family in California. I didn't wait to think about it or listen to my intuition. I didn't know I had one, or any kind of voice that mattered.

I felt important. I felt wanted. I had a reason to leave. A big one.

Was it love? I'm not sure. Excitement, adventure and escape? Probably. A man interested in me? You bet. That was all I needed to make one of the biggest moves of my life. I'd grown up basing my worth on whether or not men loved me. This time, it was enough to make me move 3000 miles away.

Sometimes You Have to Breakdown to Breakthrough

"I'm grateful for all of this," I tell my best friend over crepes and mimosas one day. Shelly's been through dating, marriage, childbirth and tattoos with me. She knows everything, and I'm lucky to have her. We met one day at King's Dominion amusement park when my then-boyfriend's best friend brought her as his new date.

We sit at lunch twenty-five years later, and she watches me shed uncontrollable tears. She's been my witness, my confidant, my cheerleader and my biggest supporter through every painful thing.

She looks at me, and I feel seen. "It's not lost on me why I'm here, living this life," I tell her, then shove a bite of crepe into my mouth between furious vents of emotion. "I had the opportunity to heal deep wounds, change my life," I say. "I don't regret any of it. But I'm done."

I come up for air after another sip of mimosa and wipe away a drop with my napkin before starting in again.

"I've learned big lessons. I get that choosing to get married and have kids are what brought me to this moment. I'm grateful to be where I'm at." I feel the words and recognize the attempt to convince myself, rather than her.

"Even the really shitty moments are okay," I tell her. She listens patiently until I run out of steam.

"I love myself more now," I tell her. "For once in my life, I actually feel worthy and confident." She smiles and nods. I recognize the acknowledgment in her eyes, and it wakes me up a little. And waking up is how I got to writing. It's how I got to healing the most painful parts of my life: the unworthiness, the shame, and the fear of never being enough.

Waking up ended up being a magic wand of transformation. My BFF would be a vehicle for that magic. She'd end up steadfast in her ability to hear my pain and love me without judgement.
There would be other important ways I'd wake up. On the treatment table. In the dojang. On the trails. In moments with my kids. But it seems there'd have to be a lot more pain before then.

My "Mom" Lecture for Helping Ease Introversion

I was the most unconscious in high school and college. Low self-esteem burned a hole inside me but I didn't really know why I felt so horrible about myself. My parent's divorce and the way we lived our lives just seemed like the way it was. I never felt in control of any of it.

When I went through my own divorce years later, I wanted to make sure my kids didn't suffer the same fate.

"Are you sure you don't want to go to homecoming buddy?" I asked recently from my usual barstool on the corner of the kitchen island. It was a year and a half after my divorce and I was trying to think back to what happened with my parents. What they said to me. How I felt. I couldn't remember anything.

My senior baby was in the kitchen to tell me about something that happened at school the week I was out of town. I, as usual, was worrying about him, thinking about all the ways I was fucked up after my parents divorced and all the years I'd spent healing those wounds. I feel desperate to not let my kids feel that way. To make sure they know their worth.

"No, I don't want to go, Mom. It's not my thing."

"Is Brett going? What about just going with friends?"

"Yeah, Brett has a girlfriend. He's going."

"No girlfriends in the picture, bud?"

"No, Mom, I don't like to talk to people." A slight pause, then he continued. "I have five friends."

"Five friends is a lot!" I smiled. But he wasn't smiling. "Everyone else knows everyone in the school, Mom."

I pressed, despite the risk of alienating him. "Will there be a senior prom?" I asked, already knowing the answer.

"Yeah, and I probably won't go to that either," he said, turning around and walking back down the hall to his room while I was still talking.

My heart ached for him. He has what I have (or had anyway): rock-bottom self-esteem and debilitating introversion. And in that moment I could feel it in my chest like I did when I was in high school. It just felt like when I'd walk the halls alone, watching all the cliques of popular girls gather around the lockers, envying the way they looked. I'm not pretty enough, I'd think.

I decided to follow my son to his room, risking his embarrassment and anger.

"Can we talk for a few more minutes, bud?" I asked nervously, starting to clean up his room as I spoke.

"Okay," he said, pulling his hands away from his keyboard and sliding his gaming headphones down around his neck.

"Are these clean?" I asked, moving the basket of laundry from the floor to my nose, then to his bed and starting to fold. "Listen, there's a trick to talking to people, to it feeling better. I was the same as you in high school. Talking to people felt like a fucking torture chamber," I said, knowing swearing would get his attention. He looked up with some interest as I continued the mom lecture.

"I was exactly like you. I was an athlete and that was okay for a while. My friends were my soccer team, like yours were from baseball," I tried to convince him. "I had one best friend," I divulged, which got him to raise his eyebrows at me.

"One, buddy! If you have five, you're doing pretty good! The thing is, you're not the only one who feels like this. You have to remember that when you're in a crowd of strangers. All you have to do is ask them questions. People love talking about themselves," I offered. I continued with a little role play, to show him what and how to ask questions.

"You can talk to people, bud. You're smart and handsome and really funny," I said, watching his eyes move up to mine again when I finished my compliment. "It's not like you sit there and say nothing when someone asks you a question. You know how to talk to people!" I repeated with a little too much enthusiasm.

"When someone says, 'hey,' you say 'hey' back. If they ask you a question, you answer it. So the trick is to ask other people questions and break the ice that way." I waited for his buy-in. He wasn't having it, so I continued, "The next time you're in one of your smaller classes at school, look around. There are people more shy and uncomfortable than you, promise. Try asking them a stupid, easy question, even if you already know the answer, and watch them come to life."

I explained how sometimes you just need someone to see you. To notice you. To make an effort to talk to you, and everything becomes so much easier. I asked him to try to get over it being all about him and to approach someone else who might need more help than he does. I'm not sure if my talk sunk in, but I was really glad I decided to try.

And God, did I speak from experience. What I really wanted to say in that moment was, "Dude, don't spend your entire life trying to find your self-worth like I did, only to realize it was up to you this whole time. Don't spend your whole life figuring out that you matter, that you're amazing and intelligent and funny and the world needs your magic."

I did talk to him about self-esteem and worth. I snuck it in there as gently as I could. I tried to get him to see it doesn't have to be all about him, that he can reach out through his own pain and fear and help someone else worse off.

"Does this all make sense?" I asked, frustrated by his silence, something I've never gotten used to. I don't remember this being a huge issue in middle school. "Yeah," he nodded.

I finished folding the basket of laundry. "I love you, bud," I said, turning to leave.

"I love you too," he replied.

I shut his door behind me and went back to my spot at the island, leaning my elbows on the cool brown granite and staring at the login screen. *There's got to be a way to help him,* I thought. *What is all this work for if I can't help my own son with the problem that's plagued me my entire life? What's this all for, if not for that?* My mind continued with desperate problem-solving chatter mixed with a wiser voice that said, *It's okay; he'll find his way.*

I believe that voice. I've grown to know it and trust it now.

I rebelled in every way possible in high school. In particular, sex became a drug for me. It meant I was worthy. I keep wondering when my son will rebel. I hope for it actually. Maybe it will help him find himself, like it eventually did me.

"What's this?" my mom demanded one day, pulling the used rubber out of my trash can. *Shit, shit, shit, I can't believe we forgot the trash can,* I thought, as I racked my brain for some reasonable response. I sat staring at the Shawn Cassidy poster on my wall and then looked at the floor. There was no response to give. "You know, Dee told me about you and Billy," my mom said, raising her voice a little.

I felt my cheeks flush and my gut clench. I'd assumed because I was responsible enough to get the pill from Planned Parenthood and cover all my bases, that this eventual confrontation wasn't going to be so horrible. I was wrong. I felt sick with shame. But I was addicted to the feeling of someone wanting me. That longing to be needed was stronger than the humiliation I experienced as I sat there with my mom looking down on me. And it was stronger than the wimpy feeling I had when Dee, a family friend, opened the bedroom door on us that night.

"You're not my mom!" I remember shouting at her when she told my boyfriend to get lost. "Come on," I grabbed his hand, and we left the house. "I don't need a babysitter," I remember saying as I slammed the door behind us.

For a long time, having a boyfriend (and later a husband) meant I was worthy. That's partly what made my decision to leave my marriage so conflicting.

"I don't know who I am," I tell Shelly over the phone one night, stepping out onto the back patio and sliding the glass door shut behind me so the kids can't hear. "I don't know what to do. Maybe I've made a mistake. What if the kids are wrecked over this?" I ask her, hoping she'll remind me why I made the decision to ask for a divorce. I feel all my worth drain from my bones. I'm back to being worthless, alone, unloved, and ashamed.

"Listen, you made this decision so you could be free and happy. You've been miserable for a really long time. You're going to be okay. Everything's going to be okay," she says.

"But what if it's not?" I demand. "What if everything goes to shit and I realize I made the biggest mistake of my life?"

There'd be so many conversations like this between the moment I asked for my divorce and the day I left the courtroom with the final papers that I'd lose count. My girl would consistently listen and remind me of my why. She'd show up when I thought I'd die. And she'd love me when I'd cancel plans at the last minute. She'd forgive some nasty words, and she'd understand when I turned down her invitations. For a year.

Reflections on Self-Loathing

Thinking back to the times I'd vie for the attention of any man who'd have me makes me ill. It feels so far from where I am now, writing this book, on the other side of that big pain, that I barely recognize that girl as me. One of my greatest fears is that I might not be any further in my evolution now. How much more do you really love yourself, I wonder. More than the night you banged your head against the wall waiting for your druggie boyfriend to come back?

Maybe a little more than that.

I'd ended up waking up a little more during my moments as an athlete. In fact, being an athlete would save me many times over, from high school to midlife.

I was a pretty good fullback in high school. Soccer was my life for a while. I played for the varsity soccer team in high school then for San Francisco State University for two years before stopping to hone in on my studying.

Being on a team gave me my sense of worth, of belonging. It was the other thing besides sex that'd make me feel important and good about myself.

In fact, my love of soccer was what got me off drugs.

I remember the turning point very clearly. It's two a.m., and I'm in the bathroom of some stranger kid's parentless house.

"Laura, are you okay?" my friend Seth hollers at me. "I'm fine!" I shout back as I roll up a dollar bill and snort another line on the counter, courtesy of Seth's brother, our local high school's drug dealer. Seth's one of my best friends, but tonight, he's my very best friend.

I'm not sure how much of my pizza-making money I spent on coke that semester. I'd get a lot of it for free, because Seth loved me when I was high. Coke was what allowed me to be the extrovert I always wished I was at school.

"Come on, we're leaving," he hollered again. But I wasn't finished.

I stood up from my bent-over-the-sink position and caught a glimpse of myself in the mirror. I grabbed a tissue for my nose, fixed my hair, straightened my black miniskirt and pulled my pantyhose up, smoothing the wrinkles around my ankles before I opened the door and smiled at Seth.

I loved me when I was high too…until I hated me. The smile was fake. This wasn't the person I wanted to be.

The next day, I walked onto the soccer field at 8:00 a.m., nauseous, dragging my purple-and-gold duffle behind me. "I feel sick, coach," I admitted. "I don't think I can play today."

"Okay, D." D was my nickname back then, as a starting fullback who was known for her ability to score from half-field. My teammates would yell,

"Deeeeeeeeeeeeeeeeeeee!" every time I tried it.

I'm more grateful for that morning than most others in my life, because I quit drugs that day.

I was done numbing myself out. With drugs, anyway. I knew that kind of high would be the end of my soccer career if I wasn't careful. I didn't want to take the risk of losing the one thing that made me feel like I was meant to be alive. The only thing, besides men, that gave meaning and purpose to my life. The moment I had to bow out of the game because I was too hungover to play was the moment I realized I couldn't risk losing my sport. I was so ashamed.

Sitting in my car thirty years later, I'm high from the adrenaline rush of my Tae Kwon Do class. I feel good. I can talk to people. I'm a good player; I kick ass most days. The high of exercise, like it's done every year for the last couple of decades, gives me power, makes me feel worthy, numbs my pain.

I vow never to quit this awesome sport. I make plans to train harder. Be better. Be a role model. Be perfect. Until I think about that night, getting high in a stranger's bathroom, and draw parallels to the pursuit of perfection I'd rather ignore.

"If It Was Easy, It Wouldn't Mean Anything"

"Laura!" My master calls me over to his table at the end of the small, rubber-mat-covered room where he sits during our black belt exams, given every six months. We're required to write an essay as part of it. The exams are a chance to remember what I'm made of. We're in the middle of sparring, but he's reading my essay and says, "I know what you're going through."

I let out an audible sigh, "Don't make me cry!" I beg. Because there's no crying in Tae Kwon Do. "Don't let it happen," he replies. He's talking about the part where I wrote about my marriage, about feeling done. Up until then, my Tae Kwon Do essays were the only place I was brave and transparent on the page. The stuff I'd written for others to read up until then had been only half-ass brave. He gets my full-on brave, and he has ever since I started my martial arts journey.

I stand in front of him to receive my promotion after nine hours of testing. I shake his hand and avoid his eyes. He knows. I don't want him to know. I want this to be easier. But he knows what I don't know: that if it was easy it wouldn't mean anything.

Deep breath. Back in my body, the only place I have any chance of doing this healing I'm meant to do. The only place I can hear the voice of my intuition and inner wisdom. This might not feel easy, but it's worth it. I'm a warrior. I thrive by being curious about uncertainty.

But I'm afraid the sport's just another way to get high. I'm afraid of going to that place again, even though I'm sure there's no chance of it. *You have to stay awake,* I say to myself. *This is the only way you'll survive. This is the only way your life will have purpose and meaning.*

Kicking's been more than an adrenaline rush. The practice requires presence. And presence is the path to healing, so long as I don't use it as an escape. Which is why I didn't worry when I found myself in class instead of home talking to my husband. I gave myself permission to do the things that grounded and centered me, in the midst of my struggles. Being able to face and do the things I can't do is the greatest of gifts. Kicking gives me that gift on a regular basis. I remember watching my classmates try to break their boards many years ago and thinking, *Oh my God, what if I don't break mine? What if I fail? What if I can't do it?*

"Discipline the mind, the body will follow." My master's quote. It's on the wall in his dojang. It's on my notebook full of forms that I bring to every class. *Yes, discipline your mind, Laura, for God's sake, quiet the voices and just do this,* I hear.

The contest in Tae Kwon Do is always against yourself. Against your mind and your fears. Always an opportunity to find out what you're made of, even if you're getting your ass kicked in the process. The day you realize it's your own ass you're kicking is amusing.

"You can't numb pain without also numbing the joy."—Brené Brown

Yep, I get it. I've taught it. *Well fuck, I want joy, so now what?* I think. I spend a lot of days asking myself questions that are hard to answer. I get high on the big questions, remember? *How do I arrive at a place where I can feel all my feelings of worthlessness and not want to numb those fuckers up?* I wonder. I hear you, Brené, but you haven't told me *how* to do this. Chocolate anyone?

If I'm going to be the brave warrior heroine of this story, my mission will have to be to break the chain of numbing. For me, my daughter, my son and their future children.

I wonder if we're born with perfect self-worth. I wonder when we start paying attention to the opinions of others when it comes to loving or hating ourselves. How do we decide to believe those opinions? If we're shown unconditional love as a child, do we have a better chance? Would we be spared from a lifetime of searching for it?

I'm remembering something from Bruce Lipton's book, *Wisdom of the Cells*, where he talks about the first few years of life as being the time of imprinting these foundational subconscious beliefs and I realize I'm fucked.

The memories of my early childhood include a moment when I sat next to my sister in my dad's Datsun 280Z, a two-seater, me in the passenger seat and her on the middle console. Dad was smoking weed with us in the car, windows rolled up. And he liked to drive the hairpin turns of Rte 1 back and forth from Stinson Beach at night. Occasionally he'd let out a cackle and turn the headlights off.

I've based my current healing dilemma on the idea that I wasn't shown the love I deserved by my father and that his words and actions gave me the message I was shit and that I'd have to prove my worth by doing and saying all the right things.
That I wasn't worthy *unless* someone else thought so. Unless they loved me, wanted me.

One night, years ago, I talked my best friend from high school into coming with me to the strip club where my latest male prospect worked.

"Hey Jenny, come on; it'll be fun!" I coax.

"Okay, I guess," she gives in. We don our best black miniskirts, show up at the club and find seats at a tiny round table in the dark. The room's dingy and crowded. A lot of other ladies in black adorn the room. They're getting more drunk as we sit there.

I'm hoping for attention and get an obligatory lap dance after waving my dollar and slipping it into his G-string. I feel excited to touch the skin at the top of his hip. Jenny and I giggle but can't think of anything normal to say, so we watch as he makes his way to the next tiny table of women.

Later, at least an hour after Jenny took a taxi home, I desperately wait by myself on the street outside the back door of the club, hoping to catch my friend on his way out. I shift from my right foot to my left, trying to lessen the pinch of the black pumps I've worn a few minutes too long, darting my eyes back and forth from the back door to the surrounding street for any sign.

But he doesn't show. I wait a long time, fully denying what's happening. I'm being rejected, I finally admit to myself. *I wonder if I can go back inside for another drink?*

I wave down a cab instead and bottle my tears until I arrive home and fall into bed, exhausted. Lying on top of the covers, staring at the ceiling, I let a few tears roll into my ears before the buzz of the alcohol puts me to sleep.

Looking back I can see that the early programming from my father left scars I noticed as I second-guessed my decision to ask for a divorce, risking being an old maid for the rest of my life. *What would a good girl do?* I think. Certainly not this.

I look back at my life with a certain amount of awareness now and realize that young woman really believed she wasn't good enough unless a man loved her. The woman looking back now asks for her freedom because she finally realizes she's good enough, worthy of love and joy, with or without a man.

I realize I believed I was whole only if someone loved me and that someone would only love me if I was perfect. I morphed myself into so many other people's definitions of perfect along the way that I lost myself. I existed only to be wanted by someone else. Before I could heal, I needed to fall in love with myself first, and that wouldn't happen for a while.

2
Awareness is Everything

"Without awareness there is no choice."—John F. Barnes

Welcome to the first and most important tool in this tool book: awareness. Staying awake and aware gives you the choice to live the life you crave. It's time to go for the joy.

The first step to changing anything in your life is practicing awareness. Waking up is about noticing how you feel, think, act, and behave, and everything associated with those. Showing up for the stuff of your life with mindful, authentic presence is how you get everything you desire. And the first step to waking up is learning how to feel the sensations in your body. It's a process and practice that'll serve you for the rest of your life.

Warrior Exercise: Body Awareness Meditation

(You'll find a great body awareness audio I recorded for your listening pleasure for at: http://lauraprobert.com/brave-healing-book/)

What you'll need: A comfortable place to sit or lie without distractions, along with a notebook, pen and timer.

Sit or lie down in a comfortable position, body fully supported. You can close your eyes or keep them open, whatever feels more comfortable. Take a deep breath and imagine you are sinking down deep into your body. What do you feel? Take another deep breath and, as you inhale, fill the front, back and sides of your ribcage. As you exhale, relax and release your body, head to toe. Bring your focus—or awareness—to the body and the breath. Notice the sensations as you relax further. Begin to clear your mind of thoughts and bring your attention to the feelings or sensations in your body. When your mind becomes cluttered with thoughts, just gently bring your focus back to the body and the breath. How does your body feel on the surface it is resting on? What parts of your body do you notice? Relax, release and make space around any tightness or places of tension. Keep taking deep, full breaths and follow the sensations of your inhales and exhales as you relax even deeper. Unclench any tight areas. What do you feel? What thoughts or judgements do you notice coming into your awareness?

Take a couple more deep breaths as you open your eyes and bring your awareness back to the environment around you. When you're ready, grab your timer, notebook and pen. Set your timer for five minutes and write. Start with, "I feel_____" and fill in the blank.

A note about the writing: There are no rules to this kind of therapeutic writing. Do not censor yourself. Do not worry about punctuation, grammar or finishing sentences. Just try to keep writing until the timer goes off. Stay connected to the sensations of your breath and body as you write. Move the messages from inside yourself, to the paper, without overthinking, analyzing or judging them. Just let your writing flow. Try not to get stuck on the prompt itself. If you find yourself stuck with nothing coming into your consciousness, then you can just write the words, "I feel stuck," again and again until something else comes. The trick is to stay in action with your pen on the page and write what you feel.

Optional: If you are working with a partner on these exercises, you can make a decision to share your writing by reading it out loud. This is a powerful exercise that brings life to your words and thoughts. I would encourage you to honor one rule in this instance: no commentary. Just read and/or listen with an open heart. Both the reader and the listener, if aware, will be able to receive the exercise as a gift.

Big Brave Question: What do you feel right now?

I returned to the hotel after a Myofascial Release (MFR) class, finished for the day, exhausted but excited about the new way my body felt after the treatment we practiced. I slid off my clothes and popped into the bathroom, ready to shower for dinner when I caught a glimpse of someone in the mirror. That someone was me—I just didn't recognize her. This phenomenon was strangely wonderful. Instead of being freaked out, I stared with wonder at the woman in the mirror. The body I saw was beautiful. It was the first time I remember ever feeling this way about myself.

The class woke me up to the beauty beneath my skin, to an energy I was radiating. To love. I started wondering what healing really meant that day and how, through awareness, I could experience more miracles.

It's all about awareness; a brave kind of awareness. The kind of fierce, unrelenting mindfulness that kicks your own ass some days. You need it; lots of it. All the time. Until you die. If you're not into staying awake for the stuff of your life, and prefer to float through life a bit numb, then pass this book to someone else right now. If you're ready to dive into the most amazing adventure of your life, read on!

You're a warrior. You're ready to do this thing with me. What're we doing? Taking the journey of our lives to feel illegal amounts of happiness. Right? But first ask yourself, what's in the way of your joy. What in your life needs healing? Your physical body? A relationship? Your sense of purpose? Your bank account? Is it your social network or community? A lack of self-love? They are all connected.

Brave healing isn't a destination or a goal to achieve. It's the journey and practice of awareness along the way.

Here's the truth about healing: it will take you the rest of your life, and some days it will suck. It means being your most vulnerable, exposing your deepest wounds, taking huge risks and making difficult decisions. It means crying, laughing, and everything in between. It requires all of you; not just the tough parts, but the soft, easy parts too.

And…staying awake for the stuff of your life will be the most incredible, magical, joyful, rewarding thing you ever do.

Healing's about realizing we have the choice to feel joy, happiness and love, no matter what scenario we're faced with. Brave healing is about making those choices in every moment of every day, for the rest of your life. It's about practicing the awareness that gives you those choices.

How do we do that? By being present, mindful and aware in every possible moment. By connecting with our inner warrior—the intuitive guide on our personal journey—we can develop the discipline of awareness and use it every single day, with every single thing that happens to us, including the really challenging or just plain awful stuff.

By making loving awareness the default of our body, mind, and soul operations system, we can feel our way into and through the stuff of our lives. Doing this gives us powerful choices. We can choose more joy.

You can use this powerful tool for everything. Our most peaceful moments and our most desperate both benefit. All moments can be enhanced by awareness, whether we're alone or in a crowd of strangers. Everything can be enhanced by awareness. From the sensations in our bodies, to the thoughts in our head, to the reactions of our spouse or the plan at work. From the grief over the loss of a loved one, to the actions making up our exercise routines, to the moments we wonder why we're on the planet.

Beware of Excuses to Play Small

Your inner warrior's the one you can rely on to take you where you want to go. That inner guide will always tell you which direction to step. It's a matter of listening to his/her messages.

I spent decades justifying my feelings of fear and unworthiness. The labels I chose to define who I am were limitations I placed on myself when I wanted an excuse to play small. I was the introvert. It's how I explained my dysfunctional fear of connecting with people.

The qualities of an introvert describing how one recharges or fills their cup are spot-on for me. I bask in solitude; feel energized when I'm still, quiet or alone; and have noticed that socializing in large crowds of people tends to drain me rather than fill me up. What has changed is my ability to find joy and even excitement in expressing my real, wild self to others, even big groups of others.

The work I've done to wake up, know my worth and transform my fears has healed the part of me that used the "introvert" label as a shield. I remember one day about ten years ago, before I knew the real me, when the mother of one of my daughter's friends caught me in the hall at the kids' preschool to chat. "Are you in sales?" She asked when we got around to talking about our professions. I laughed out loud, then stifled it when I realized she wasn't kidding.

The "me" that people were seeing surely wasn't introverted. So, what was happening? Where was the disconnect between the "me" I felt inside and the "me" others saw? *Sales?* I thought. Not over my dead body (or my painfully shy, humiliated one, anyway). That day, I began to peel off some of the heavy layers covering my soul. Someone had seen my light shining out, and I couldn't hide anymore. *Who was I becoming?* I wondered. And what was I supposed to do with her? And even if I kind of liked the new me, how would others react?

The more worthy I feel and the braver I am, the more extroverted I look it seems, but I still don't vibrate with the labels. It doesn't feel like extroversion to me now. It feels like loving myself. It feels like finally being comfortable in my skin, enough to relax and enjoy other people. It feels like confidence in making choices serving my health and well-being. It feels like a healthy "I don't give a fuck what other people think" attitude.

What a relief. Feeling this way's so much more expansive, inspiring, exciting and fulfilling to me. It has opened up my world in huge ways, brought me connections in my personal and business lives that have been nothing short of miraculous, and enriched my creative projects by adding collaboration as an option. I'll never go back.

Can I have all that with introversion too? Sure, but what if we drop the labels and just feel the feelings? Feeling what's going on and using the awareness to tap into the moment and what it feels like was the way I moved into the current state of what I'll call the "Brave Expression of Me." Is it extroversion when I feel amazing and connect with people from that new energy? I'm not sure I care. I just know that what happens from that space is magical.

If it hurts to be introverted or you're using it as a label or excuse, then examine what's going on. Understand that being yourself can and should feel good…even awesome. This isn't about how you fill your energy cup; it's about how you feel concerning expressing yourself and your gifts to the world. If that feels tight, constricted, limited or painful, ditch the label of introvert and go for what's holding you back. Explore and face your fears. That's the shit you have to heal. And all healing is, in this case, is giving yourself permission to be yourself.

Begin uncovering the layers smothering your soul and making you feel unworthy of expressing your ideas, opinions and talents. Let your discomfort be the way your body speaks to you, letting you know introvert's just an excuse you've been using to stay in your comfort zone. Get comfortable with feeling uncomfortable for a while.

Maybe the introvert/extrovert story is more like a yin-yang one. We need to find the balance between the two sides of ourselves and thrive inside the flow of that balance. If we identify with labels, it begs taking a look at redefining ourselves. If we're attached to the label and use it as an excuse for our behavior, maybe we should explore that. We're so much bigger than mere labels.

Who Do You Think You Are?

You don't heal or evolve without awareness. "I'm pretty happy. I don't think I need to heal anything," I hear you say. Humor me. Dig deeper.

Are you in love with your life? Are you doing something every day that you love so much you lose track of time? Are your days filled with mostly joy, ease, flow, creativity and passion? Or are they plagued with worry, doubt and fear? Love these big questions.

Don't think you deserve an easy, happy life? Think again.

"Who do I think I am? I'll tell you who I am. I am a child of God, just like anyone else. I am a constituent of this universe. I have a right to collaborate with creativity because I myself am a product and consequence of creation."— Elizabeth Gilbert

"I'm just a worrier," you say. "I've never been able to relax." Since you're used to living a certain way, are you resigned to that being your reality? Can you dwell in the possibility that there might be a way to reduce your anxiety and experience a freedom you've never dreamed of? Can you entertain the idea that the way you've always been doesn't doom you to having to stay that way?

To feel inspired to go after something more, you must feel hope. I want to give you the hope that anything you want to feel in your life is possible. Even if you've lived your whole life without it. Even if you don't think you deserve it.

Guess how that's going to happen? Awareness. Awareness IS your inner warrior. Watching yourself and your thoughts is going to allow you to change your perceptions and voilá: hope enters, stage right brain.
Awareness is just that: observing and feeling yourself, your thoughts, your sensations and your emotions like you're watching (and feeling) a movie.

You must step outside of yourself to do this. You must realize there's part of you that knows what's going on, hears every thought, feels every pain, is aware of every reaction, response and belief. You must step outside of yourself and look in at what's happening.

My favorite author on this subject is Eckhart Tolle. His books *A New Earth* and *The Power of Now*, shaped the way I understand awareness. *The Big Leap* by Gay Hendricks brought it all to another level by taking everything I know about awareness and helping me learn how to use it to figure out where I was sabotaging my own life. My favorite healer in this realm is John F. Barnes, the founder of JFB Myofascial Release. John teaches healers from all over the globe how to use and teach awareness as the foundation for mind, body, spirit healing. And my Tae Kwon Do master reminds us, "Discipline the mind the body will follow."

I'm applying and integrating what I learned from these masters into my life. And I'm seeing results. Time to pay that forward.

There's a part of us—the inner warrior—that knows what we need and how to get there. We have to learn her language, which comes to us in the form of feeling, sensation and emotion…things that many of us were taught to ignore or resist. The body's the GPS system of the soul. Because your inner warrior talks in feelings, emotions and sensations, there are messages in the way sadness, anger, guilt, fear and shame feel in you. There are messages in the way hope, joy, love, bliss and happiness feel in you. Are you listening? What can you feel?

Bottom line is that if you're not awake and aware, and if you don't show up for the stuff of your life, you'll miss the boat to bliss on its way to someone else. Show up and catch the boat. I'm going to show you how to learn the language of your inner warrior; to find, nourish and activate your own healing power and start on a journey to find yourself and what you love.

Take my hand. Be brave. You're not alone.

Are You Paying Attention?

I remember sitting at one of my Tae Kwon Do exams a few years ago. We were finished with the physical part of the test and were all sitting on the floor cross-legged, listening to our master talk. The speech at the end of a test is always something I pay attention to.

It's taking some effort to relax and concentrate after the five or six hours I've spent giving every ounce of energy I have. My legs start cramping, but this moment holds a special opportunity: to hear the wisdom of my teacher.

I let his words move through me, and this particular night they're meant especially for me. Because I'm present in my body, and paying attention to the energy of pure love with which he's speaking and being, I experience a small amount of healing right then. I feel heard and seen. His words do that for me.

Looking around the room to see if anyone else's paying attention to what just happened, I think, *Did you hear what he just said? Do you feel the love?* But that's the thing…my moment's mine. I know others soak it up like I do, but I wonder about those who are asleep for it, and hope they wake up and feel so they can heal too.

There're so many opportunities in your everyday life for this kind of experience that it's hard to count. The trick is being present for them. What's happening in this very moment you're in that you can be more present to? What're you feeling right this moment that you can tune in and listen to?

It's all about awareness. Every moment. Every day. Every morsel of your life's there for you to seize, each a tiny possible miracle. It's in the way you discipline your mind and observe and respond to every thought, sensation and stimulus. Every sound, word, taste, smell, touch and event holds something you can use for reflection and healing. For perspective. For transformation.

Let how you feel be your discipline. Pay attention to how you feel in your moments. Some will feel tight and some will feel free and easy. Let those feelings be a compass to guide you to your next move, your next thought.

Warrior Exercise: Your Intuition is a Feeling

Grab your notebook and pen again. Take a moment to breathe, relax and drop down into the physical tissues of your body. Relax, release and soften, making space around any tightness you feel. With every exhale, let go a little more. Practice clearing your mind and feeling your body for a few deep breaths.

Writing prompt: Take a piece of paper and draw a line right down the middle of it so that you have two sides. You're going to be making two lists, side by side. At the top of the left side write the words "Hell Yes!" Make sure to put the exclamation point! And at the top of the right side, put the words "Hell No!"

Set your timer for five minutes and start by describing how the "Hell Yes!" feels in your body. What does it feel like when something you're thinking, believing, doing, experiencing, hearing, etc. is a full-on yes inside you? What does your body actually feel like when this happens? Make a list of descriptive words down the left side of the page. Try not to stop writing until the timer goes off.

Now I'd like you to do the same thing for the right-hand side of the page, and the "Hell No!" list. How does it feel when something isn't right, or is a no for you? What does your body feel like in this scenario? What does it feel like when you're thinking, doing, or experiencing something that's a "Hell No!"? Set the timer for five minutes and make a list of words that describe this.

One note about a feeling of confusion or uncertainty. Instead of being unclear, uncertain or confused, realize that these feelings are usually a "Hell No!" There really isn't a grey area when it comes to the way your body feels. It's time to be clear about these messages, so I'm going to help you by letting you know that feeling uncertain or confused is the way your body is telling you no. And you can even make a separate list of what your body feels like in a confused state and compare it to your other two lists. The descriptions should be interestingly similar to your "Hell No!" list.

Big Brave Question: What are you saying yes to that's really a "Hell No!"?

What you've just created is a cheat sheet for yourself about the language of your intuition. When the body feels a certain way, it's a message to you. By checking in with how you feel, you'll be better able to know if you're choosing things based on what aligns with the yes or the no. What feels good to you is what aligns with your desires and with joy. What feels bad to you does not. In fact, making choices despite the feeling of the "Hell No!" over and over will eventually become painful.

Feeling is healing. What you feel helps you know what's right for you. What you feel helps you know whether or not you're living life on your own terms, aligned with your own soul, or living according to everyone else's rules and opinions. What you feel is your intuition. By practicing feeling, you'll be learning this new, important and life changing-language. You can trust what you feel.

One last note about awareness. If I ask you, "What do you feel?" and you say, "I don't know, I don't feel anything," then could it be you're numb? People don't like that word. But it describes how we are when we want to avoid feeling. We numb up in a lot of different ways, for a lot of different reasons. For now, I want you to just practice feeling what you feel, even if it's nothing. Feeling is healing. Your ability to feel is your superpower.

In the next chapter, we'll explore how to feel doubt, anxiety, insecurity and fear and how feeling those things can be a compass for living your wildest dreams. Get used to feeling doubt, anxiety and fear just like any other sensation in the body. These tools will be a game-changer in your life.

But before we get to those tools, let's do one more exercise to help you with your big why. Your why, the reason for living fiercely alive and doing this work, is what will carry you forward on the journey. So if you don't know who you are, what you want or why you want it, nothing else is going to matter much.

Warrior Exercise: Who Am I and What Do I Want?

(You'll find a great body awareness audio I recorded for your listening pleasure here: http://lauraprobert.com/brave-healing-book/)

What you'll need: A comfortable place to sit or lie without distractions, along with a notebook, pen and timer.

Sit or lie down in a comfortable position, body fully supported. You can close your eyes or keep them open, whatever feels more comfortable. Take a deep breath and imagine you are sinking down deep into your body. What do you feel? Take another deep breath and, as you inhale, fill the front, back and sides of your ribcage. As you exhale, relax and release your body, head to toe. Bring your focus—or awareness—to the body and the breath. Notice the sensations as you relax further. Begin to clear your mind of thoughts and bring your attention to the feelings or sensations in your body. When your mind becomes cluttered with thoughts, just gently bring your focus back to the body and the breath. How does your body feel on the surface it is resting on? What parts of your body do you notice? Relax, release and make space around any tightness or places of tension. Keep taking deep, full breaths and follow the sensations of your inhales and exhales as you relax even deeper. Unclench any tight areas. What do you feel? What thoughts or judgements do you notice coming into your awareness?

Take a couple more deep breaths as you open your eyes and bring your awareness back to the environment around you. When you're ready, grab your timer, notebook and pen. Set your timer for five minutes and write.

Writing prompt: If there was nobody left to offend, upset or disappoint, who would I become?

A note about the writing: There are no rules to this kind of therapeutic writing. Do not censor yourself. Do not worry about punctuation, grammar or finishing sentences. Just try to keep writing until the timer goes off. Stay connected to the sensations of your breath and body as you write. Move the messages from inside yourself, to the paper, without overthinking, analyzing or judging them. Just let your writing flow. Try not to get stuck on the prompt itself. If you find yourself stuck with nothing coming into your consciousness, then you can just write the words, "I feel stuck," again and again until something else comes. The trick is to stay in action with your pen on the page and write what you feel.

Optional: If you are working with a partner on these exercises, you can make a decision to share your writing by reading it out loud. This is a powerful exercise that brings life to your words and thoughts. I would encourage you to honor one rule in this instance: no commentary. Just read and/or listen with an open heart. Both the reader and the listener, if aware, will be able to receive the exercise as a gift.

Big Brave Question: If who I am is not what I do, then who am I?

3
Are You Insecure?

Rest Into Its Wings
by Laura Di Franco

I blamed everything on you
It took me a while to see the truth
What you took from me long ago
Is no longer under your control.

I decide who I am
I decide when to speak
I'm worth just as much
As anyone else, any fine week.

Here you are to teach me lessons
For all I know you were sent from heaven
To help me discover all my real power
You had to be an ass and make me cower.

You chose the role to help me grow
I just thought you hated me so
Now I'm grateful to be able to forgive
Put the puzzle in place and learn how to live.

Without you there to teach me to fight
I would have stayed small, not seen the light
I would have slept through each glorious day
Just hoped on dreams, instead of finding the way.

When I look back at the resentment and pain
I see it's all really my gain

I can let go of blame and set myself free
Looking to love for a better way to be.

I'm taking back my voice and feeling my power
Thank you for giving me a chance to discover
The pieces of myself that I'd forgotten about
Possibility, potential, passion, no doubts.

Now in these difficult moments of need
I can give back to you from a heart that is free.
I can find the love that was lost for so long
Because now I know nothing truly was wrong.

I can give from a place of warrior love
From awareness and choice and help from above
Maybe you will feel the very same thing
Show up for love, and rest into its wings.
~~
One of the things our body feels is the sensation attached to our thoughts. Doubt, fear, worry, shame and uncertainty have feeling in the body. These feelings are similar to the "Hell No!" feelings. Making a connection between thought and feeling is how you begin to have some freedom and control over your life.

"If you want to clean house, you first have to see the dirt."—Louse Hay

Without awareness of the thoughts and beliefs and the way those feel in you (the dirt), you won't have a choice to respond in a way that serves your desires, dreams, goals or big why.

Your inner voice might say, *Are you sure about this? You know what happened last time.* The negativity paralyzes you with doubt. This voice is famous for asking, *"What if..."* and always defaults to the worst possible scenario. It tells you that you're a fraud and reminds you of every past mistake and failure. It tries to make you believe you're just not good enough, smart enough, skinny/pretty/lucky enough to do what you want to do.

I sit looking at my big, wooden table covered with mix-and-matched bowls and cups filled with pens, markers and paints. The leaves on the tree in my view out the sliding glass door boast three different colors at once, and in that moment, I'm sure about the magic of the universe and my place in it, convinced my dreams are meant to come true.

How do you know? My mind is happy to trash the serene scene. *What if nobody's interested? Who cares about healing anyway? They just want a quick fix. You're writing the wrong book. You're better off writing about how to get rich quick; that's what everyone cares about. Plus, you don't have enough experience to teach anything to anyone. Nobody's going to listen. Nobody cares.*

I'm quickly not so sure anymore, and my writing stops. *This's all a waste of time,* I think. *I should go back to my day job.*

"It's easier to be confused," Robin, my acupuncturist, said to me after I told her how I'm feeling about my marriage. I've been seeing her for over ten years. She knows everything. "It's easier to be confused because you don't have to make a decision," she continued, making me squirm. Robin always pushes me to the truth quickly. My sigh and lack of response gave her permission to continue. "Getting clear about what you want means you have to make a decision and that's harder than staying confused and stuck."

She's right. It's hard to admit what I already know: I want more than what I have, and I'm back to feeling ungrateful and bad about myself for it. It's easier to be confused and just stay discontent and stuck. It means I don't have to speak up for the things I want and need in my relationship, which just feels easier. I don't have to make any changes. I don't need to make waves. There might be consequences to that.

"You're in your own little universe half the time," my now ex-husband complained later that same night. "I don't matter in this family." He's only partly right. He matters, but speaking up is so painful for me that I'd rather just do things on my own. I'd rather ask for forgiveness than permission. I don't want anyone else's opinion. I've given so much of myself up in the past, there's nothing left for him.

I sat on the warm, wooden deck of a huge sailboat in the middle of the Caribbean with my girlfriends from grad school. We lounged in the smell of salty seas mixed with Banana Boat and soaked up the sun, while sipping pink rum punch and spying the cute guys next to us. The blue of the sky dancing with the mixed blue-greens of the water was heaven.

"He's kinda cute," my friend elbows me with a glance toward the back of the boat. "Yea," I agree, sitting there staring at my friend's boobs.

Hedonism is an all-inclusive resort in Negril catering to those who love to party. There's a regular beach and a clothing-optional beach. My girl-friend, who had just up-leveled her Goddess status with new boobs, wanted a place where she was sure to be able to show her girls off. Hedo-nism was the place.

My suite-mate talked three of us into this Spring break in Jamaica and I'm not sure there was full disclosure from my girlfriend about the nature of Hedonism before we arrived. Those were the pre-internet days, so I never looked it up. In the span of a few days, she had changed her mind from Hawaii to Jamaica, and the rest of us were just along for the ride.

By the time we arrived, it didn't matter; we were off on an uninhibited adventure that would change the course of my life. The dictionary defines fate as "the development of events beyond a person's control, regarded as determined by a supernatural power." Not sure what kind of supernat-ural power was working that week, but it's when I'd meet my husband.

I naturally gravitated to the people—two guys—who still had their clothes on. My girlfriend and her boobs were busy sunning themselves and gathering attention on the big deck at the bow of the boat. My bikini was as close as I'd get to showing skin. (That day, anyhow, but that's another story.)

"Hey," I said to the guy near the bar as I stared down at my pink drink. I, along with everyone else, it seemed, was having trouble ignoring my friend's boobs. They were spectacular.

The boat pulled up to a gorgeous, sapphire inlet and anchored there. We were offered another rum punch before jumping off the gang plank to swim to the edge of a thirty-five-foot cliff. One by one, we jumped into the water and swam to the edge where there was a ladder to the top of the cliff. We climbed, arriving at the top and hoisting ourselves onto the ground above.

One after the other the drunken sailors ran off the edge of the cliff and cannon ball jumped into the water thirty-five feet below. That was, and will be, the only time I ever experienced free fall. I landed on the water (which felt surprisingly concrete-like) with my limbs flailing and my mouth open in a scream. I don't remember making any sound, though. I remember falling into the ocean, and the feeling of that density, the return of my weight against the water and stomach to my body, being a big relief.

While the others excitedly swam back to the ladder for more, I, on the verge of tears, swam back to the boat, where the helpers pulled me aboard. Thankfully, I had enough wits about me to notice my bikini top had slid off my breasts with the force of the water and adjust it before arriving at the boat. Someone pointed at at the blood dripping off my chin, and I raised my fingers to my mouth, confirming their worries after seeing the blood on my fingers. My frenulum had torn in half. You can find your own frenulum by sticking your tongue up behind your top lip. Feel that sharp, thin piece of skin that connects your gum to your lip? Mine ceased to exist at that point. Frenulums do grow back, though, and mine is quite normal today.

Odd side note: in his younger years, my son would end up having a frenectomy, a procedure to laser away an extra amount of the tissue when it impeded proper closure of the two front teeth. Go figure. I try to disassemble mine, and my son ends up with too much.

Needless to say, I was done cliff jumping for the day, but thankfully the trauma wore off. "Hey, can you look at this and tell me how bad it is," I said, pulling up my top lip and enjoying flirting with my future husband on the sail home, hoping to attract a fair amount of sympathy from him. The rum punch didn't hurt. I was so much better when I was high.

The next day, my girlfriends and I found our two new guy friends from the sailboat and lined up at the beachside bar for shots. "Hey!" I said, sliding up next to the guys, "What are we drinking?" During the day, the attire was bathing suit casual, so we drank in our suits, a little sandy and a medium-amount buzzed, waiting for the next concoction the bartender had in mind.

Most of the week, the dress code was the smallest amount of clothing we could get away with. Lingerie night at the disco was interesting; it reminded me of the running race in San Francisco called the Bay to Breakers, a seven-mile run from the bay to the ocean, where the attire was, well, optional. When my sister, and mom and I ran it the first time, we dressed as cows. We were accompanied by many fully naked people. Naked except running shoes, that is.

I'd noticed another woman talking to my new prospect (in that flirty sort of way) the day before, and the competition put me over the edge. I would win. (Since we ended up married for twenty years, complete with two healthy kids, I would say I definitely won. Never get me in competitive mode. It's a little scary. I think the first time I stopped being competitive was after I had kids and decided that letting them win felt better than winning.)

"This is called Kiss Me Quick," the bartender announced as he topped off our shot glasses. It was some combination of vodka and Kahlua. All the drinks had names like that, perfectly chosen by those dread-locked Rasta bartenders with their deep, sexy, steel-drum accents, for just the right moment. This was my moment. My guy and I drank and kissed. Just a small peck of a kiss, but I knew it was the beginning.

"Hey, let's sign up for this!" my friend said later. It was the "Deserted Island Rum Punch Picnic" day, or something like that. I have no idea what that excursion was really called, but if I had to name it now, knowing what it was, the word "orgy" would be included, along with the words "drunken fool" and "breasts."

We sailed out to a small island where the staff had prepared a jerk chicken BBQ for us with, of course, pink rum punch. There was so much rum punch that day, I began seeing double. The game of the day was some sort of strip poker circle. We all stood in the water, and truth-or-dare kind of questions accompanied lots of drinking, until there was naked- ness. If you got the question wrong or didn't want to drink, you had to remove a piece of clothing.

As modest as I was, I still ended up with my top off at some point. I don't totally remember the rest. Maybe that's a good thing. It didn't take much to get me drunk, and if there's anything about alcohol I can be proud of, it's that I never improved my tolerance. I'm still a light weight. That last sentence makes me laugh out loud at this screen. It's the little things.

My prize and I would continue to court each other for the next several days—despite the other red-headed girl's failed attempts to try again— until it was time for his friend and him to leave, a couple days before me. "I'll call you when we get back," I promised. This wasn't going to be a four-night stand. I wonder if that bartender knew just what kind of cupid he was being that day. I wonder how many couples get to say, "At Hedonism," when asked where they met. I watched the guys get on their bus to the airport and dreaded the next couple of days I'd have to wait to talk to him again.

The trip as a whole wasn't particularly one to brag about. I still have trouble answering the question, "Where did you two meet?" The friends who know us used to use it against us most times, considering how con- servative my ex-husband is. They loved to see the reaction. "You met at Hedonism?" They wanted to know the details.

Our tropical love affair turned into a one-and-a-half-year long distance relationship followed by a twenty-year marriage. I've spent a lot of time wondering if I pushed my husband into everything that's our life now.

I've doubted it all.

I did everything I was supposed to do, according to what I believed. Found a career I loved, got a job to support myself, fell in love, got mar- ried, had two kids and got a dog. Living the dream. I moved through my life from one big accomplishment to the next, still high, but this time on the thrill of achievement. When one thing was done, I moved on to the next, hoping to fill up the still-deep hole in my soul. Nothing was working. So much to be grateful for, a life so full, yet still empty. How could it be?

You've Gotta Love Yourself First

There should be a few classes taught in school. Along with Self Esteem 101, How to Manage Your Finances for New Grads, Communication for Dummies, and How to Develop Healthy Relationships, first and foremost there should should be Self-Love for the Beginner.

When it comes right down to it, all the success in the world won't mean a thing unless you really care deeply about yourself, recognizing your worth as equal to every other human being and living creature on the planet. There's nothing that makes you less worthy. Nothing.

"I think we have to love ourselves fiercely. Like a lioness protecting her cub. Like we are about to be attacked by a marauding gang of thugs...out to make us feel bad about ourselves. With joy and enthusiasm and entitlement. We have to love ourselves with pride and dignity. We have to aggressively love ourselves. We have to practically stalk ourselves, that's how much energy we need to put into this. We really do need to discover our inner Viking and wear our shining armor and love ourselves as bravely as we ever thought possible." —Liz Tuccillo

When you let this sink in, the opportunities become vast. You really can be anything you want. Your parents weren't lying when they said that. No dream is out of reach. No, not even becoming an astronaut is out of reach. When you take life head on with a positive attitude and a large amount of enthusiasm, there's nothing you can't do.

Allowing the opinions of others to squash your enthusiasm must mean you've put them above yourself in the worth department and that their opinion trumps your own feelings and intuition. That's the biggest mistake I repeatedly still make in my life: allowing fear of the opinions of others to stop me from doing something I really want to do, listening to my intuition, and/or from speaking up and expressing my desires.

"There's nothing wrong with loving the crap out of everything. Negative people find their walls. So never apologize for your enthusiasm. Never. Ever. Never."—Ryan Adams.

All I could think when I read this quote the other day was FUCK YES! It's been the story of my life to let negative people influence my enthusiasm. I must take full responsibility for this. I can't change what others think, say or do. I can change how I react, how I let it affect me, what I say or do in response, and how I believe and behave in support of my own dreams in the future.

I'll add Psychology 101 to that list of required courses in school. When you learn about the psychology of people, you begin to learn ways to live and respond that allow you to not take on other people's shit, to build healthy boundaries. Honestly, if we can't understand how our own minds, bodies and spirits work, how will we get around in this life without feeling at a huge disadvantage?

Sunday Morning Yoga
by Laura Di Franco

This is my church
Smooth wooden floors
and walls
Feng Shui'd
just for me.

Glass stained
with the green
of trees
and sounds
of birds.

Confident believer
up front
ready to give me
the secrets of life
and body mind.

This is my church
my pink mat pew
and holy water bottle
by my side.

These people
their seeking spirits
lift me up
and I am home
as me.

This is my church
not because
I don't believe in God.
But because my definition
is bigger.

~~

When you start to define yourself, your world and your God in terms of something bigger, you realize there are no right definitions. You realize everyone can have a different one, and they're all right.

Another "supposed to" activity in my childhood was going to church. I was baptized Catholic, as was my father. Gram was a severe Catholic. I drove her to mass now and again, not ever feeling comfortable sitting next to her on the pew. The should's and supposed to's of church didn't feel good. There seemed to be so many fucking rules and definitions of what's right. Gram would say that in the hands of my parents, we weren't brought up religiously, like we were supposed to have been; church wasn't really a thing for us, except for the obligatory Easter and Christmas. As soon as I could, I vetoed all of it. The moment I was able to decide for myself, my decision was to stay far away from church and its rules about how I should behave.

The rules of religion can be a needed relief in some instances. Particularly with ceremonies and traditions around death. In some religions, what you do when someone dies is spelled out to a T. Nobody needs to worry about what to do, or figure out the wishes of the deceased, or decide what the right thing in the situation is. It's written in the rules.

You follow the rules, and you don't have to wonder. I think the traditions people have followed and the rules they obey in this particular instance are a relief, as they allow the family space to grieve, rather than have to worry about arrangements.

My profession's paved a path, as a healer and seeker, to being able to explore spirituality. Every time I think of the gal in my high school career center who pointed me toward physical therapy, I feel immensely grateful that she sparked a light in me leading to healing. This exploration is the path to dreams coming true. To living in full expression of the magnificence we are. To allowing life to be lived through us, our passion and enthusiasm to light others along the way. And to do all of it through love. That's the God I want to hang with: the one who makes love his way of doing things. Rules or no rules.

When my mom married the son of a Lutheran minister (my second step-dad), I figured I must be— for real this time—going to Hell. He would tell us so. Going to church meant forgiveness of your sins. Without that relief, you were doomed.

I went a few times for my mom. It made her happy; it made her husband happy. Doing things out of obligation would get old, though. After my kids were both baptized in the Lutheran church, for my parents, I let go of needing to do anything more to make them happy in the religion department. I'm not sure I totally let go of the guilt I still felt for disappointing them, though. Guilt is a tricky, destructive thing.

I was spiritual, whatever that meant. Problem was, to my mom and step-dad, that didn't mean I believed in God. My church was the yoga studio, the dojang, the forest. It had nothing to do with believing something because I was told to believe in it. It had to do with following my heart, getting in touch with my inner wisdom and intuition, and listening to the pulse of life in every moment. I'd been on a healing, spiritual journey for a while, devouring every book on present moment awareness I could find and listening to every message that said the expression of your truth was a path to freedom.

This stuff made sense to me; it resonated inside me physically. And I was getting better at listening to that voice. Church and religion did not resonate. Too much guilt and not enough love. Too many different people fighting over who's right. In parts of the world, even killing each other over it. I will pass on that kind of God. If what most religions agree upon, that God is love, made that agreement their sole teaching, we wouldn't be killing each other over it. There has to be a bigger definition.

I think I have an idea what that may be, but we'll get to that in a moment.

Below is an email from my mom to her pastor, copied to me, as she checked in from her mission trip in Cambodia in 2016:

"Still recovering from tour of Tuol Sleng museum yesterday. Looking forward to church today, and meeting the folks at Rehab House. So many stories Pastor. We visited with a young ten year old who begged at our table at lunch. Multiple rapes. Turns out Andy knew her so she visited with us. I can't explain the pervasive sadness of their predicament here. But so importantly, I feel God here. He has to be, or one could not survive this."

What was my mom feeling? The possibility there's a love big enough to heal this, I think. This's a truer, and much grander, definition of God. A feeling inside. Yes, Mom, you're feeling God. God's inside you. You are God.

Mom will be sixty-eight this year. She'll come back from Cambodia changed, given a perspective that'll shape every moment she has thereafter. The amount of courage it takes to grow in this way is huge. People will judge you and your dreams. It's your choice whether or not to listen. Whether or not to let them influence your enthusiasm. Your choice to believe their definition of love, or your own. And it's your choice whether or not to live your life in pursuit of that love, or stay a spectator on the sidelines. Mom has witnessed love in the middle of a true nightmare. The only thing that could possibly wake us up is love.

Some people wonder if the Universe has a plan for us. I've wondered the same many times, along with wondering if I'm doing it right. Some are content thinking that when we die, that's it, our one chance is up. Some talk of a never-ending spirit choosing the next life based on being able to help others, learn a lesson, or help another person learn a lesson. Others report that we get to choose the meaning of our lives, that there's no pre-determined meaning or purpose.

There is a lot of freedom and a crap load of responsibility in that last idea. If we make up the meaning, then we not only determine the meaning of our life but we also have the power to change it any time we feel like. If we determine the meaning, it is up to us to find that meaning, to discover our purpose of being on the planet.

What if we never do? Does that mean we've failed? According to who?

There's no time like the present to begin making your dreams and passions come true. It doesn't matter your age or stage of life. Now would be the time. If fear is trying to talk you out of your dreams, recognize that voice as something outside of yourself. Clear your mind. Listen to the other voice, the one coming in shades of ache and elation. Of sadness and joy. Listen to the one making your body tingle and buzz. The one making it feel as if it was going to explode. Follow that voice. Deeper. Yes, now you're on your own path to your dreams. Don't let anything stop you. You got this.

On Asking Big Questions

I'm thinking back to one night when I joined my now ex-husband on a walk with our dogs. A two-mile loop that's a usual running loop for me. I know he wants company, motivation to exercise, and I for once have the energy to go. We haven't had a lot of time alone to talk and this's my chance.

We make it about three quarters of the way through the walk in silence. I'm frustrated. Finally, presented with a rare opportunity to talk, and we don't. The anxiety's building in me and by mile one and a half I can't take it anymore. I go for the big guns. "So, do you ever wonder why we're here on this earth, like what this whole life thing is about?"

It was a mistake to hit him with a question like that. I don't know what I was expecting. I have to admit, I didn't expect the "no" answer I got. I was sad. Shocked, actually. I had so much excitement in me about finally being able to discuss one of the big questions of life with my husband, and I was totally blindsided by the response.

His "no" didn't keep me from expressing my views on the subject however, sharing that we take life so seriously and how we're really meant to experience joy and love. That I spent a lot of time wondering why we're here, what our purpose is and how to fulfill it. That I saw the magic. At that point, my voice had dulled a bit, knowing what I was saying could be falling on deaf ears. Was it enough to know he was listening, even if he didn't really get what I was saying? It didn't feel like enough.

By the time we arrived home, we were in an argument about finances. Somehow, expressing my joy for life and quest for meaning and purpose always ends up in the need to ask permission to spend money on some of the things that help me on this path: continuing education that supports my growth as a healer and courses and retreats that support my growth as a human being are the things that lift me up and fill my soul with inspiration. They're what I know I need to fulfill my purpose, which is to teach what I know and inspire others.

If my husband doesn't understand that underlying desire, he won't understand the motivation I have to spend that kind of money. He'll always think it's a waste of time and resources. This's a predicament for me. How do I continue reaching for my dreams and also respect him and where he is on his journey? Is it possible?

Dollar, Dollar Bills, Y'all

I have had a cushy life, for which I'm very grateful. And I'm fully aware I need to be careful what I wish for. So I'll just say I believe in the power I have to manifest the income I need to keep reaching for my dreams in the form of my personal growth, and to do it independently of my husband, is totally possible.

I have always had a deep desire to be able to support myself financially. To be able to afford the courses I want to take, without having to ask for permission. To have control over that part of my life. Because I went from school, during which I was supported by my parents and student loans, to living with my husband, my situation was always one of combined income. Before my divorce I'd never had a chance to be on my own financially and test the waters of my own capability. I'd always relied on other people, or known because of the cushion of my husband's income, I didn't need to worry too much.

Not that I haven't earned my own money. When I turned fifteen-and-a-half, probably to the day, I obtained my work permit so I could begin earning money. My biggest goal was buying my first car, but then I needed money for gas and to spend doing stuff at the places my car took me. My first job was at Pizza Hut, where I bussed tables. I worked in another pizza place, at an ice cream store, and as an aerobics instructor before graduating from college and getting my first real career job.

By the time I got married, I was used to earning my own money and was proud of being able to do so. Somehow, though, it was never enough and the belief I could never make enough to do the things I wanted to do remained. I was afraid I'd always have to ask other people for the extra money I needed to feel happy. I was afraid I'd never be successful or be able to count on myself. I was afraid I'd never be good enough on my own.

Some amount of insecurity is normal. But how I felt seemed to take up a lot of real estate in my mind, keeping me paralyzed and in a vicious cycle of doubt and fear. Looking back, I'm aware that requiring outside approval for everything caused me to then need it…for everything. Rather than trusting my own sense of what's right, I looked to other people for the security and acknowledgement. I'd soon learn that looking anywhere but inward would prove futile.

Part of brave healing is creating a security and trust from your own intuition. It's about awareness, of both the sensations you're having and of your thoughts. In the next chapter I'll show you how to up-level your awareness by watching those thoughts and aligning them with what serves your highest good.

4
Cultivating Confidence

"Discipline the mind, the body will follow."—Master John L. Holloway

The next tool of awareness to continue your brave healing involves gaining a deepening awareness of your thoughts, along with identifying and dealing with your inner critic. If feeling is healing, then being aware of the thoughts you entertain is super-powered healing. Differentiating inner critic from intuition will happen with this level of awareness, and this's where you can begin to shift from paralyzed to powerful in your life. Mastering your thoughts and the emotions linked to them is how you move toward joy.

Let's get this chapter going with an exercise.

Warrior Exercise: Breathing With Fear

Get comfy, either seated or lying down in a room with as little distractions as possible. Make sure to have your notebook, pen and timer nearby. Relax into your body, letting go and softening into your seat or bed, and close your eyes. Begin to clear your mind by bringing your attention to the breath. For this exercise, we're going to breathe through the mouth for both the inhale and the exhale.

Feel the inhale as it comes into your body. How does the air feel as it enters your lungs? Relax more with the exhale, letting your whole body soften and let go. Bring the breath deep into your belly button area…let the belly fill up with your inhale and feel it flatten with your exhale as you let go even deeper.

Feel the breath as it fills the belly and expands your ribcage. Notice any sensations in your body as you breathe. Are there any areas of tightness or tension? Soften and let them go with the exhale. For the next couple of breaths, imagine filling up the front of your body at the belly and the back of the lowest part of your ribcage at the same time. The diaphragm can expand in all directions. Let go deeper with the exhale, releasing your entire body.

Now, breathe with the intention of filling up and expanding your side ribcage. As you bring the air deep into your belly let your body expand out the front, back and sides all at the same time. Then completely let go of all tension on exhale. You don't need to push the air out, or force anything, just let your body exhale and release.

Take a few more full, expanding breaths, each time releasing your whole body as you exhale, letting your awareness and attention stay with the sensations of the breath.

Notice what you feel, where you feel, and how you feel with the breath. Let's breathe for a minute or so now, connecting the inhale with the exhale and releasing more with each exhale. Don't be afraid to make noise with your breath. Now, slowly relax your breathing, bringing your attention back to the room and your surroundings, and slowly open your eyes when you are ready. Grab your notebook, pen and timer. Set your timer for five minutes and without stopping, finish the sentence: When I find my voice and speak up my truth_____.

There are no rules to this kind of therapeutic writing. Do not censor yourself. Do not worry about punctuation, or finishing sentences. Just try to keep writing until the timer goes off.

Optional part two: If you are working with a partner on these exercises, you can make a decision to share your writing by reading it out loud. This is a powerful exercise that brings life to your words and thoughts. I would encourage you to honor one rule in this instance: no commentary. Just read and listen with an open heart. Both the reader and the listener, if aware, will be able to use the exercise and receive it as a gift.

Big Brave Question: If you could feel fear in your body, recognize it as a compass pointing you in the direction of the truth, what would your truth be?

When I started competing in Tae Kwon Do in 2006, all hell started breaking loose in my mind. The fear, the anxiety, the voices in my head…they all tried to paralyze me. I showed up for the competitions and did okay until it came time to enter the "holding" area where competitors waited to be called for their event. By the time I arrived there my heart would pound and my legs would begin dying a slow death. *I can't do this,* I thought. *This feels horrible.* My mind continued to create a visceral sensation of being paralyzed. Not great when you're about to start a kicking match.

Looking back at those moments, I realize a big part of me was still trying to be perfect, still trying to achieve and win to be worthy. The "not good enough" thoughts took over. It would take a fierce discipline and awareness of my thoughts to begin to change the default pattern I was in. I put so much pressure on myself to perform well that I could barely perform at all.

My master stood there, a rock in my world, and never judged. I started to feel worthy in his presence whether I won or lost, whether I was good or bad that day. As soon as I started catching my thoughts of doubt, worry, shame, or fear ahead of time, I could begin to control how I reacted, in any situation, not just in the dojang.

Being able to use awareness to notice your thoughts and the feelings associated with them is one of the biggest keys to healing and transformation. When you start to learn the difference between your inner critic or sabotaging voices and the voice of your intuition or soul, you begin to have an internal GPS system directing you to clarity and confidence.

To help you learn more about this practice, I've broken down awareness into warrior spirit and the warrior mind.

Warrior Spirit

In Tae Kwon Do, we practice the tenets of courtesy, integrity, perseverance, self-control and indomitable spirit. It's this last one that describes the warrior. It's what I was talking about in not giving up. It's a commitment to your own life and goals, no matter what happens. Having a warrior spirit is one of the secrets to healing and living a joyful life.

Warrior spirit is a particular form of awareness.

Part of the indomitable, warrior spirit is practicing awareness and being unwilling to waver from this path. It's a discipline. I see discipline as something you do every day, whether or not you feel like it, because you know it will help you reach a goal you desire. I see the spirit of the warrior as the very essence of your life, not something you are because you think you should be that way, but because you realize it's the only path to making your dreams come true.

A warrior spirit lifestyle is a deal breaker. You just know there's nothing that'll change your mind. When you're infused with warrior spirit, there's no alternative. You're awake most of the time and very few things can put you back to sleep. There's no choice but to live brave inside of awareness because you always have the feelings backing up your actions. It's a barometer letting you know what'll pull you in the direction of bliss or take you backward into your self-imposed jail. Usually once you break out of jail, you'll do anything not to go back there again.

Warrior spirit is courage, self-worth, determination, discipline, purpose-driven action, reflection, awareness, vulnerability, heart-centered living and vision.

The skill you're perfecting is awareness, in all the forms we practice. Every moment can be experienced through awareness. Alternatively, anything in any moment can be ignored, suppressed, resisted, stuffed down, brushed over, judged, belittled or devalued. So there's awareness and there's your reaction to what you're aware of. When you're tied up in reaction, you're in jail.

Notice your thoughts and feelings without reacting to them and feel how things shift. Notice them and choose better, healthier ways to feel, and watch your body and soul transform like you never thought possible.

And...it takes a crap ton of courage to live aware in all your moments. Hence the "brave" in brave healing. Awareness is easy in the "good" moments but hard in the "bad" ones. When you practice warrior spirit, you learn not to judge your moments at all, even and especially the bad ones. Every moment becomes meaning-neutral, and you feel how it affects you inside. From that awareness, you get to choose how you respond. Choice (and freedom) come from awareness.

Let's do another exercise to help you practice understanding that inner critic voice that paralyzes you.

Warrior Exercise: The Inner Critic

Practice dropping into your body more quickly now. I've led you through connecting with your body in the previous exercises. Now I'd like you to practice getting there faster. Clear your mind, drop into your feeling senses by taking several slow, deep breaths, and relax, release, soften and feel. Realize you can connect like this at any moment, as quickly as you desire. When you're feeling relaxed and in your body, grab your notebook, pen and timer. Set your timer for five minutes and do this writing prompt following the same rules (no rules) as before:

The messages my inner critic tells me are_____.

Remember the optional exercise of reading your writing out loud, either to yourself or a trusted friend. Giving a voice to your words is a powerful way to heal.

During one of my first jobs as a physical therapist, I was promoted to the center manager position and was responsible for several employees at this big company. One of my employees was having trouble with our corporate management and, in my opinion, was being treated unfairly. "Liz, listen, Maria was only doing what she thought was best for us. I don't think this kind of disciplinary action is warranted." I stood up for Maria and, due to my actions, was demoted from my manager position. I was then forced to take a staff therapist position split between two other locations, both an extra thirty minutes from my home. I was devastated. I felt betrayed.

"I can't believe they did this!" I cried to my husband that night. I'd just returned to that job from my maternity leave and was juggling a full-time job while being a first-time mom. Part of me wondered if they were discriminating against me. I spent many days in tears after that, dumb-founded by my boss' reaction to my (what I deemed noble) actions. My self-worth plummeted. I spent months wasting time trying to figure out how I deserved a demotion. I couldn't move on.

"I just can't see how this could happen. I'm a great employee; dedicated, hard-working. I'm good at what I do!" I tried to defend myself with my husband for months afterward, while I worked in the other two locations and started hating it.

"Hey, did you see this?" My husband handed me a postcard one day about starting up my own clinic by partnering with a new company. Long story short, I pursued it and ended up co-owning three successful therapy clinics shortly after my demotion. If I hadn't gone through the pain and torture of my "bad" event, I would have never pursued the new opportunity. It would have never even been on my radar.

Bottom line, I believe everything happens for a reason. Even the bad stuff.

We don't always see the reason when we're in the middle of the crap. We can judge events as good or bad, but we cause ourselves undue stress by doing that. Truth is, we don't know what the outcome of most moments will be. We aren't totally sure if it will be positive or negative. We have to trust that it's part of our path for a reason. We have to surrender to it. Of course, we don't have to do anything…we can stay stuck in our patterns of complaining, bemoaning and resenting, and stay in our jail cell too.

Dr. Wayne Dyer talked about this in his book, *Excuses Begone!* He said if you can't be 100 percent certain something will turn out positively, but you also can't be 100 percent certain it will turn out negatively, you have the freedom to pick either of the two thoughts. "Why not select the one that will work for the highest aspirations you hold, rather than against them?" He asks us.

From awareness we get choices and freedom.

It sounds simple. It may not be easy. We know what to do, but we don't do it. We already have the answers, but we're stuck in old patterns of thought and behavior. What will it take to change? What will it take to do things differently? To be brave?

Overcoming the Need to be Right

"You're basically telling me I'm an idiot!" I scream at my husband. He's just finished criticizing the way I'm running my business, and his words cut like a knife and bring up all kinds of feelings from my inner three-year-old. Stupid's one of them. Instead of stepping back from his words, feeling the feelings, and responding in a way that expresses what's happening inside of me, I go for the throat, raise my voice, and make every attempt at "winning" the argument and being right.

This tactic hadn't worked yet, and we'd been married for almost twenty years at that point. You'd think we'd be open to a new way, but we keep reacting out of protecting our little, scared children inside, and that's unconscious behavior. Right there's the wound we're out to heal, but instead of practicing being aware of it and using compassion to change the way we communicate with each other, we keep ripping the wound open and waiting for it to stop bleeding. It scabs over and we pick at it until we can't stand it and rip it off again.

"When you say that about my business, I get this feeling in my chest and feel so stupid and unworthy," I should have said. "I want to listen to what you have to say, and I'd love for you to help me, but when you say it that way, I just react." When I slow down long enough inside my own thoughts and feelings, stay awake, and stay brave enough to be vulnerable, this kind of response usually gets a much raver review. But it takes a lot of awareness, energy and self-restraint to speak this way, especially when I'm triggered.

Another helpful response is, "Sometimes I make bad decisions and you're probably right about this. I feel so powerless when I hear criticism."

This isn't an attack, it's a cry for help. Instead of triggering someone's defense mechanisms, I can ask for their wisdom and help. This's a response that comes from me observing my own thoughts, feeling the associated feelings, keeping everything meaning-neutral, and then communicating a description of those actual feelings. It's hard, but it's really effective. The warrior spirit has to take over. I have to be okay with being wrong and feeling vulnerable. I must want to be happy more than I want to be right.

I have to tolerate the feelings coming up in a severe trigger and stop myself from defending. So difficult yet so necessary to create a change in the long-standing pattern I have, we have, of bad communication.

Sometimes it's not the outside world that's crushing our spirit, but more the internal voices. Internal voices can be even more cruel. Part of this fierce awareness we're cultivating is about the voices in our own head— the inner critic.

Sometimes "inner critic" is a fair name for this voice, but most times, "evil, self-sabotaging demon" fits better. This monster doesn't require any sleep or food. It's there, night and day, and it's immortal presence makes you feel like seeking out your local priest for an exorcism.

My exorcism came in the form of a book by Laura Munson called *"This Is Not the Story You Think It Is: a Season of Unlikely Happiness."* In it, she talks about giving her inner critic voice a name. *A name!* I thought. *Brilliant!* There's something about giving that voice a name that quiets her down.

When you recognize the voice as outside of yourself, and then give it a name (not your own), you can start listening to it with more objectivity and curiosity. You don't have to listen to it all the time, and you can start to analyze it a little more and decide if it's helpful or not. You can stop believing what you're thinking. This gives you a pause button, allowing more time for deeper awareness.

This little trick was a game-changer, a profound shift in my awareness that's given me the power to un-stick myself when I feel paralyzed. It enhanced my awareness ten-fold, helping me realize that the thoughts going through my head weren't all necessary or helpful. In fact, most were just an unworthy, scared little girl trying to protect herself, worried about what others would think, scared about being bad, and basically terrified of being herself.

When Martha (my voice's name) speaks, I hear her right away and shut her down. "Thanks for trying to protect me, but I got this," I tell her. The more I practice hearing her and feeling the sensations in my body that accompany her messages, the better I am at knowing when it's her. There're only rare moments now when she wins, which means I fall asleep and listen to her and let the fear paralyze me. More often it only takes a second to realize it's her and move on to something more productive. When I add self-compassion to the awareness, the voice dissipates even more quickly.

Listening to those messages, both the voice and the feeling inside, is one of the biggest ways I know when to act (or not) on them. If something's a "no," there's a tight, constricted, choking, sick feeling in me. When something's a "yes," there's a light, easy, warm, fun, joyful feeling. These are the voices of your intuition. The first step is to recognize the voice, feel it in your body, clear your mind and breathe with the feeling.

The next step is to express it, in whatever way you want or need to, depending on the situation. As in the example with my ex-husband, if there's someone else involved and you're having a discussion, you can express this by describing how you feel. Slow everything way down. Observe and feel before you speak. This's very difficult if you're used to shooting out the first thing that comes to you. Keep a warrior spirit and remember, vulnerability is your strength.

Let's do a follow-up exercise from the last one. Do a quick read of your last writing exercise, beginning with "My inner critic messages tell me," and then follow up with this:

Do a quick body check-in, dropping deep inside, clearing the mind and connecting with the breathing for several slow, deep breaths, relaxing more and more with each exhale. When you're ready, pick up your notebook and pen and write down your inner critic's name.

The name can be a real name of someone you know, or another name that just comes to you and doesn't necessarily make sense. Don't censor yourself here. Write down what comes to you. Now go back eight paragraphs and re-read them. See what comes up.

Warrior Mind

You must know you have shit to heal. We all have some. It's recognizing it that's difficult, especially if you've grown up in the world of "I'm right and you are wrong" like I have. I think I've spent my whole life defending my "right" way, even thought that way was based on what everyone else told me.

What do you feel right about? Where are you unwilling to change? What're you unwilling to feel? What triggers you? Where does your resistance show up and take over? What in your life feels tight, limiting or like a jail? These are big neon signs pointing to possibilities for healing and transformation.

"Right" is defined by each person. The person, decides what right is based on his own personal opinion or filter of what he thinks is right, which's what he was taught by his posse (family, teachers, coaches, friends, therapists, society). So, what makes something right? Who gets to make the rules? The president? The pope? Your Uncle Fred?

For now, let's exclude the example of laws made to protect us from harm. I really want to talk more about the "right" we grow up with from parents, coaches, teachers or other family, friends or elders. If your person isn't the "law" why do they get to make the rules? Who says their way's the right way for you? If you've been following someone else's rules for a while, how's it working for you? Part of the warrior mindset is starting to wake up to where your thoughts and beliefs come from in the first place.

At one point I brewed with resentment over this, over everything and everyone else whose rules I followed. Over having to do things I didn't want to do. Like the laundry. There came a point where I dumped all of that on its head by saying things like, "Wow, I'm so grateful I own all these clothes. What a gift it is to be able to afford these clothes. I love doing the laundry." Don't laugh. My laundry resentment once caused me to boycott it for everyone in my home but me. That was a fun week. (Not.)

Boycotting the laundry seems petty, but it was where I had the control. And rules are about control. I've learned the rules themselves really aren't what matter. It's your attitude that matters. Resentment or bitterness vs. gratitude and love.

I realized I'd never expressed what was bugging me. Nobody knew I was really pissed about having to do all the laundry. That was self-imposed. I had to learn how to speak up and ask for help and stop assuming everyone else would read my mind and pitch in.

My shit comes in the form of never giving myself permission to express my voice or speak up. It's a feeling of unworthiness, something I'll discuss in more depth later. It includes a feeling of dread about the consequences that would come from saying the bad or wrong thing.

In my adult life, I managed to follow everyone else's rules and then came to a point of being resentful of not living my own life, on my own terms. Why did I do that? Because without awareness, I had no choice. I wasn't letting myself feel anything.

As soon as I started feeling, thinking things through, understanding where my misery was coming from, and changing my beliefs and actions, a whole new world started opening up. I figured out what needed healing, discovered my triggers and could begin to look at and change my behavior.

Everything's in your mind until you get into your body. We're taught to think our way into and out of every predicament, problem and decision.

Some big questions:

What if there was another way to be?

What if we didn't believe everything we think?

What if there was no right, but only what is?

Byron Katie does some fabulous work on this topic. Her book, *Loving What Is*, is a remarkable journey into reality. It always amazes me when I manage to wake back up to what is and discover how my mind was trying to fool me and how my inner critic was quick to attack.

There's the mind that's a constant barrage of voices (we've talked about the inner critic version), and there's the mind that comes from what we sense. Maybe it's easier for you to think of left brain/right brain, but this gets confusing, so I want to talk about it in a different way. Most people have judgements about left brain/right brain from what they've been taught. I want to redefine this for you so you aren't stuck with an old, outdated definition.

To heal, you have to identify what you sense and then think about it.

You have to trust what you feel more than believe what you think. If you ignore what you feel, your thinking's one-sided. If you integrate the two, you have the best chance at healing.

When you think about the left brain being the analytical, judgmental, planning brain and the right side being the intuitive, creative, feeling brain, it's easy to judge them, right? We think it needs to be one or the other, that one is better than the other. You're both. It's about your awareness. Everything's about awareness. Even the way your brain works.

Healing's about transforming pain and fear. It's about waking up in the morning and feeling good and excited about your life. What's your shit? Why don't you feel good? Is it a pain or injury? Is it a difficult relationship? Is it a feeling of lack of purpose? Is it feeling like you are not living up to your potential? Is it daily anger? Resentment?

Figure out what your stuff is and what beliefs you have about it so you can start to see it for what it is and begin to use awareness to transform the negative to positive, to move the energy. You have to start by being willing to be wrong. It's going to feel like crap at first.
You've got to get comfortable feeling uncomfortable.

If you can't see something or understand you have certain beliefs about it, you're asleep. Everything's meaning-neutral. Reality is what is. You're giving the meaning to your life and every single event, in every moment.

Conquer Your Perfectionism

Another form of shit I've had to deal with is perfectionism. You're nodding your head now, good. Go back to the idea of who defines "right" and substitute "perfect." It's the same problem.

I remember running up the steps of my grandparents' house at the end of the quarter. "Here's my report card, Gram!" I said, shoving it in her hands before I was two feet inside the entryway. I would wait for her to count my A's and then go find her purse. I was paid to be perfect.

Years later, I sat in the office of my first job as a physical therapist. My supervisor, Sarah, came in and closed the door behind her. *She doesn't want anyone to hear this,* I thought. *I must have done something wrong.* I imagined the worst-case scenario for my performance review (a.k.a. adult report card). I was taught that straight A's was the goal. When Sarah explained all my "Needs Improvement" areas, I felt completely worthless, and stayed depressed for weeks. I would get my cost-of-living pay increase but wasn't "perfect." *I must suck,* I thought. My inner critic was full-blown.

Perfect's one of those things defined by someone else, who learned it from someone else. Just like being right, it's subjective. If I spent all my time ensuring straight A's but didn't have any time to pursue my creativity or social life, would that be perfect? Perfect has a cost. Sometimes the cost of perfect is too high. *I* define perfect now.

In a world driven by perfection (just ask any parent of a high school junior applying to college) we're forced into the stress. Don't have straight A's, perfect SAT scores, three extracurricular activities (including a sport), volunteer experience and experience playing an instrument? Too bad, you're not perfect; we'll pass.

"I think he needs to get involved in another activity," my husband said of our son one day with the assumption I'd be the one to make that happen. "If he wants to get into a good school, he's going to have to do it," he continued, "it" meaning be perfect and do everything our son's supposed to do to get accepted into college. And not just any college. The perfect, good college.

"In the big picture, does it matter where he goes, as long as he ends up doing something he loves? Isn't it good work experience that will land him a good career and give him the opportunities he wants, rather than the name of the school?" I defend.

"Yeah, but it's the school that will give him the good work experiences," he retorts.

"I disagree," I say, wanting desperately to not have to force my introvert son into the computer club just because his dad thinks he needs it on his college applications.

"Sometimes I think you just like to pick fights with me," he responds.

"Sometimes I think you always think you're right," I say.

You can see where this's headed, right? Right. Nowhere.

It makes me sick to think about this. At the time of this writing, my oldest will be a junior in a couple years. He's cool. Not perfect. Smart. Not a genius (but close). Funny. Not a social butterfly. Plays baseball but spends the rest of his time playing video games. Wonder if the world will see his worth, his creative side, his ability to figure things out, put things together, see solutions to the world's problems.

I'll tell him he matters, no matter if he gets into his first-choice college. Will he believe me? Will he remember it's his passions that count? That he can do anything he wants? Be anything he wants? Will he choose something he loves or something the rest of the world makes him think he wants? I wonder what shit he'll have to heal. We all have some.

Yours is in your mind. It's real, but it's what you think. When you can start seeing it, feeling it, and recognizing the way it prevents you from living in love and joy, you can heal and transform it.

Healing's complicated. Truth is, the mind body soul is a complex inter-connected system that can be severely and permanently damaged. Healing's relative to the situation. One of the most powerful tools to creating change and healing is recognizing the way we think about it. If we think it's possible, it's possible. If we think there's no chance, guess what, there's no chance.

Brave healing has to do with the way you set your default mindset about everything in your life. The way you think affects everything. If you constantly entertain thoughts about your pain being incurable, causing you to stay hopeless and resigned to your situation, then chances are your pain will stick around.

"If you have physical pain, you can choose to feel hopeful or you can choose to feel fearful."— Esther Hicks

If you believe the negative messages coming from people around you, you'll have less chance at healing. Choose who you spend time with carefully, especially if you have some healing to work on.

The idea of changing your thoughts from negative to positive is simple, but the reality is that it takes a warrior to monitor the day-to-day (sometimes hour-to-hour) sabotage happening. Changing your default mindset about health, healing and happiness will require you to think, believe and behave differently. It'll require you to stay awake to the stuff of your life constantly, without excuses.

Brave healing happens by adopting persistent positive thoughts. When you don't settle for negativity, doubt or resignation, creating a support system with people and environments that lift you up, you'll be surprised by the magic you can manifest.

My life seems to reflect this teaching in most areas. I wake up and go to sleep grateful for everything that's part of my amazing, blessed life. When my shit surfaces and my mind pulls me into that small box, I remember to sink down into my body and feel what's there. I remember to move into a feeling space and recognize that what I feel (sad, depressed, angry, anxious) is a result of the thoughts I'm letting into my head.

And then I let my focus shift to the physical environment around me (usually pretty calm and uneventful if I happen to be lying in my bed relaxing under my white cotton sheets) and give myself permission to drop any negativity from my mind. I choose a healthier, more feel-good thought. It's that easy.

When I practice awareness, there isn't much that can pull me into the pit anymore. I've learned to slow the thought train way down and recognize the triggers. I know my old patterns are what create the desire to react or defend. I remember I'm seeing through a unique filter that can cloud my reality. I choose to remember that my reality isn't necessarily true. I'm learning to trust my intuition and follow the messages my body sends to guide me. I'm learning that my inner warrior can always be trusted, and when doubt creeps in it's because I stopped listening and trusting.

Brave healing involves dwelling in possibility rather than always doubting. It's about staying positive and on purpose, aimed at what fills you up and brings joy, no matter what anyone else says is possible or true.

Brave healing's your only job. It's the way we'll change the world. And it's okay to have big goals like changing the world. It's necessary.

Big Brave Question: What else is possible?

5
Are You Afraid?

The Center Of The Ring (inspired by the work of Brené Brown)
by Laura Di Franco

I'm gonna wake up
To the stuff of my life
I won't play small
I'm gonna do it right.

I'll feel what it's like
In the center of the ring
Get my ass kicked
And show up again.

Because it's no real fun
To watch from the crowd
Wishing I was there
Shouting out loud.

I'm gonna play big
Hear my roar
I'll shine out my light
Give a little more.

I'll save seats for those
Who aren't ready to play
Realize their fear
Gets in their way.

I'll walk to the center
Of that great big arena

Feel what it's like
To really be seen.

I'll fight my best fight
Speak my full truth
Write my deep thoughts
Connect with you.

Because when I play large
I win the prize
A life full and rich
Among the bright stars.

The best part's when
You catch my star light
Meet me in the center
Help me to fight.

Alongside each other
We shine so much brighter
What we had alone
Multiplies infinitely together.

A powerful force
Of Warrior Love
Now let's build our team
From those seats above.

Wave to your friends
And critics alike
They all want to play
They all want to fight.

Help them wake up
Help them play large
Help them show up
Even when it's hard.

If they can't take the heat
And you're all alone
Show up again
Show them how it's done.

I want to play
I'd rather stand tall
I will play large
Even if I fall.

Because if there's one thing
I've learned to trust
Being seen, playing big
For me is a must.

The center of the ring
Waits for the warrior
Come, take my hand
We'll kick ass together.

~~

For much of my life, I heard a voice in my head saying things like, *You'll fail, so why even try?Better to just keep quiet, lie low. You don't know what you're talking about, so don't say anything. What if they don't like you?*

This voice was fueled by my ultimate fear: the fear of being myself. I'd worked out a scenario that went something like this: *If I do or say _____, people will think _____, and that will mean I really do suck.* I was always craving approval. If others liked me, then I was worthy.

I went from avoiding raising my hand in elementary school to being too afraid to ask for a raise at work to not being able to talk to my husband about our marriage. The fear of confronting someone or feeling the shame of saying something wrong and being rejected paralyzed me. I decided early on that it was safest for me to stay quiet and do what I was told, always. When I thought about expressing my opinion or speaking up and asking for what I wanted, I felt a chokehold on my throat. I couldn't breathe, let alone speak. I wouldn't risk feeling humiliated so instead of playing big, I stayed small.

My fear was born in childhood; it grew exponentially when I was eight and my parents divorced. Afterward, I became quieter, as a means of survival. I thought the divorce and the anger I felt around me must have been my fault. In order to not make things any worse, I tried never to disagree with or talk back to my parents. I also tried not to be too loud, boisterous, or enthusiastic, which seemed to irritate Mom and Dad. To avoid making them angry, I tried to be a perfect, good girl. Maybe this seemed the safest way to be with them and the rest of my family. Maybe I thought it would make them happy. Either way, I did whatever I had to do to feel loved, no matter if it made me happy or not.

Squelching My Fears to Avoid Angering Others

In the years after my parents' divorce, my sister and I spent weekends with my dad and grandparents. Dad took up sailing as a hobby and was motivated enough to start racing his 27- foot sailboat in the San Francisco Bay. My sis, age six, and I were the crew for many of those practice runs.

We spent much of our time in Sausalito at the dock where the boat was berthed. I remember using pieces of salami and mortadella as bait for the crab traps. Salami was the crabs' favorite. My sister and I loved to roll up the slices, take small bites at several strategic locations, and then unroll our meat snowflake masterpieces. Sometimes it would look like a face, so of course it would turn into a meat mask. We'd squeeze the stinky deli selections in between the trap wires and lower it off the dock with a rope.

Face down on our bellies, we'd stare past our rippled reflections in the water, watching for movement. I loved being on the dock, feeling the warm, bumpy wood under me as I hung over the side and waited for just the right moment to snatch up the trap and claim my prize. Wrapping the boat rope around the cleat on the dock in that pretty figure eight was my specialty. I was proud I knew how to do it. Those moments in the fresh air, salty breeze grounding our little kid cells, were awesome.

The time on the dock was bliss, but that all ended for me when we got on the boat with my dad and headed out into open water. I hated sailing. As we picked up speed, my sister and I would hang onto the white rubber-wrapped wire railing, our knuckles wet and freezing cold. We would lean as far forward as possible to balance ourselves at the bow and ride the huge swells, our legs clenching the fiberglass hard from the knee down. I was terrified of falling into the bay, which I knew had sharks.

When Dad tacked the boat, the boom would swing hard above our heads and we'd scramble to the other side, trying not to slip or lose our grip. We were too small to help sail, and too big to join Dad at the helm without being in his way. The sideways deck or the stifling cabin below were our only choices. I moved back and forth from the boat's dungeon cabin to the deck in hopes of finding a position that would make me less seasick. It never worked, even with taking Dramamine® to combat motion sickness.

So we held on, without life vests, praying for the moment Dad decided he'd had enough and turned back toward the dock. We listened as he laughed at us from the helm. Only when we got closer to shore, when the sails would come down and Dad would start up the motor, would I feel the knot of terror in my belly melt away in relief.

This fear around water started when I was even younger. Growing up, my family and I lived in twelve to fifteen different homes and apartments, some of which had swimming pools. I liked to ride on my dad's back in the pool, him the horsey, me the cowgirl. One day I climbed aboard, and he grabbed my ankles to anchor me to him and started swimming down. It happened too quickly for me to take a deep enough breath, before my head went under.

Underwater, with my ankles strapped to his sides, I couldn't breathe and panicked. I started kicking my legs, struggling to break free, but he didn't let go. I pounded on his back, until he finally let go and I made my way to the shallow end to escape, gasping in between sobs.

For a long time, I would think of that episode and my chest would get tight with fear. I would try to make it go away through rationalization. "Oh, he didn't know what he was doing, Laura," the voice in my head would say. "He didn't realize your head was under water." "You are fine. Stop crying." That voice made me feel like an idiot.

Eventually I learned to say, *Fuck that voice.* I knew it was preventing me from expressing my true feelings and from protecting myself. It took decades for me to get to that place, however. For most of my adult life, I'd try to rationalize or fix most of the painful events in my past rather than owning what happened to me, forgiving those who hurt me and moving on. I let those events define me.

To this day, my showers last less than three minutes, even when I shave my legs. "Water is a spiritual medium," I hear my coach, Torrie, say to me. Spiritual medium my ass... I'll take solid ground, thanks very much.

On that sailboat, in the pool, and throughout my childhood, the fear inside me felt tight, constrained, impossibly restricting. I was so fearful of making trouble that I never spoke up. I was afraid to say, for example, "I don't wanna go on that boat!" I didn't want to upset my dad.

My fear going into adulthood felt the same way: paralyzing. When I'd think about speaking up— with anyone—I'd feel a boulder in my throat and tightness around my heart. I was still afraid to share my true feelings, even when I knew doing so was exactly what I needed to do to ease the pressure in my chest. I didn't dare speak up for fear that what I'd say would be wrong, bad, or worse: I'd be punished or maybe even die. I was still staying quiet to survive, even though it was becoming more and more painful to do so.

I spent decades justifying my feelings of fear by hiding behind labels. "I'm just an introvert," I would say to anyone calling me out for being shy. Deep down, I knew I wasn't an introvert, but I was too scared to show more of my personality.

Because I was so fearful of doing anything wrong or saying the wrong thing, I was devastated if I drew any negative attention to myself. There was an incident during college, for example, that left me traumatized for years.

One day, I stood surrounded by classmates in a small room in our undergrad kinesiology class as the professor gestured to a large contraption. "This new-fangled machine is the Kincom. It's used to measure strength," he said. The professor stepped on a footplate that locked it on his side. I looked down at the footplate on my side, thinking it was unlocked, and stepped on it just as he had done. As the giant machine slid a little on the floor, I realized with horror that I'd actually unlocked it. "What are you doing?!" my professor shouted at me as he ran over and stomped on the footplate again, no doubt trying to save the machine from being wrecked.

In the end, it was me who was wrecked. Slithering behind my class-mates and out into the hallway, I leaned my back on the cold, white tile wall and tried to shove my heart down out of my throat. Humiliated, I decided not to rejoin the class that day and instead let that memory glue itself in my heart for twenty-five years. This was a small moment taking up a big space in my soul…triggering me decades later whenever I felt like I'd screwed up in front of others.

I'm sure my professor continued teaching the class and the students just went back to listening. Me? I spent years embarrassed by the memory. It was a long time before thinking about that moment didn't conjure up the same visceral reaction.

That same fear made its way into my marriage in multiple ways. Because of my relationship with my dad, I was afraid to be vulnerable with my husband (or with any man). In any interaction with him, I needed to be in control. If I felt myself ceding any power, I would clam up and shut down. I wouldn't be myself in those moments, for fear of him taking that self away from me.

"You're in your own little world, and it's like I don't matter," my husband said to me one night after a long argument about how I didn't know the "proper" way to discipline our children. "Well, you're never here to help, so I have to figure it out on my own," I defended. "Why doesn't how I feel matter to you? Do you even care what I think?" he continued, unaffected by my defense. Inside, I felt stiff, unyielding and unable to come up with any reasons for not including him in my decisions about the kids. I was paralyzed by a feeling I couldn't place or name. I wasn't able to speak rationally about this. I only knew what I felt: threatened, suffocated and stubborn.

After years on this journey, I came to realize my fear existed in the thoughts and beliefs I was holding based on past experiences. These thoughts and beliefs had become a prison, holding me locked in my own head.

Back then, my fear was crippling. It routinely triggered a fight-or-flight reaction in me; I would either fight by giving some quick reactive story about how I was right about something and start a never-ending argument, or I would flee, like I did after the kinesiology incident. Neither was a healthy way of living: they stole my freedom and my joy.

I didn't realize, though, that fear would end up being my greatest teacher. When I finally realized I could overcome my fears, I stepped into my power and started using fear as a compass to move me in the direction of my desires. Fear wasn't there to torture me, I learned. It was there to show me what to do; it became my compass.

This was never more apparent than after I started practicing the martial art of Tae Kwon Do. What started as an effort to bond with my young son at the time turned into one of the greatest transformations I would ever experience: the one from timid soul to warrior goddess. I began learning that fear wasn't always something I had to run from. I realized I could face it, explore it and ultimately overcome it. With awareness the feeling of fear turned into a compass, pointing me in the direction of the things that could lead me to my biggest dreams.

Using fear in this way helped me work through the question that plagued me for most of my life: am I good enough? We'll examine that self-created jail cell shortly. First, let's talk about allowing your fear to guide you. In the upcoming chapters, we'll start to explore and unravel fear and create tools to help you use it as your own compass.

Included here are some questions designed to prompt reflection on how fear plays a role in your life. Begin to think about the questions below and refer back to them whenever you feel fear creeping up on you. Ask yourself:

- Who are the people and what are the situations in your life that trigger fear in you? What happens to you when that occurs – how does fear feel in your body?

- When you think about your past, can you make any links to your current fears? Do you remember any times your flight or fight response had to kick in for your survival? Do you feel yourself returning to that mode today, even when there's no real threat to your safety?

- When you are experiencing fear, do you feel stuck, defaulting to the worst case scenario, or do you feel like you have options?

- Have you tried to deal with your fear? What are the ways you've done so? What's working?

- Can you use your life—everything up until this moment—as a compass to point you in the direction to help you overcome fear? Where does that seem possible? Impossible?

- When you take the story out of the feeling, what happens?

"Inquiry naturally gives rise to action that is clear, kind and fearless."— Byron Katie

Asking these big questions helps you start to use awareness to transform the fear. Your story matters. Every bit of it. And, at the same time, none of it matters. What we can do with our story is realize it's a thought about our past. We can understand how we lock ourselves up in our own heads and throw away the key. When we understand the trigger, we can begin to explore how to detach and how to choose new thoughts, beliefs and actions that serve us instead of sabotaging us.

Today, when I'm afraid, I know that facing it, shutting down the paralyzing voices and then taking swift action is the way through the fear. In the next chapter, I'll give you the how-to for those powerful tools.

6
Fear as a Compass (a.k.a. Having Fun with Fear)

"Sometimes the bravest and most important thing you can do is just show up."— Brené Brown

On the journey of life, fear can often feel paralyzing. If we're afraid of something, we tend to shut down, stay quiet or flee. It feels safer. But what if we used fear as a compass to point us in the direction of healing and transformation? What if, instead of fleeing, we showed up for the stuff of our lives and said, "Bring it on!"

Imagine how liberating that would feel.

In fact, let's do an exercise now to practice bringing this freedom into your life.

Warrior Exercise: Transform Your Fear

Before you do this exercise, consider that how you feel when you're afraid is not so different from how you feel when you're excited. In both cases, you feel energized, but with fear, you may feel out of breath, out of control. By becoming more aware of when you're fearful, you can work on feeling it, breathing with it, and letting it motivate instead of paralyze you.

The first step is to recognize when you're defaulting to your mental story around what you feel— the narrative you come back to again and again that rationalizes what you're going through. Instead, try to clear your mind and come back into the feeling by itself. Are you short of breath? Are you warm? Cold? Learn to move through the feeling without judging it.

Now let's try the exercise itself. Grab a notebook, pen, and a timer and set them close by. Find a comfortable spot to sit or lie down where you can relax without distractions. Close your eyes and begin by taking a few deep breaths. Arrive in your body and connect with your feeling senses.

Now imagine something that you want to do but are afraid to do. It could be something you'd like to say, an activity you'd like to try, or a professional goal you'd like to accomplish. Take a few moments to imagine this scenario. How does it make you feel? When you have a sense of your reaction to it, take another deep breath. Scan your head, neck, shoulders, chest, solar plexus, and abdomen. Where does the feeling of fear show up in your body? What does it feel like? How big is it? Does it have a temperature or color? What shape is it? Recognize that the thought you had is connected with a feeling, and that feeling, just like all other feelings, is just a particular sensation inside of you. See if you can describe it, without analyzing or judging it. Give yourself permission to feel it and breathe with it for several minutes. Take as long as you need.

Now begin to imagine yourself doing the thing you are afraid to do. Visualize what your body is doing, what you are saying, the environment you are in…and feel the sensations. Feel what you feel, but see yourself doing it anyway. What happens inside of you? Are you able to finish the task, accomplish the goal? Or does the fear paralyze you? What if you could take action regardless of that feeling? How would that look? Imagine yourself feeling the fear and taking the action anyway.

Continue to breathe deeply as you imagine being able to feel the feeling and at the same time take the action you want to take. Spend some time with this so that you can experience it fully.

Take a couple more deep breaths as you open your eyes and bring your awareness back to the environment around you. Grab your timer, notebook, and pen. Set your timer for five minutes and write. Start with, "If I wasn't afraid, I would_____" and fill in the blank.

There are no rules to this kind of therapeutic writing. Do not censor yourself. Do not worry about punctuation or finishing sentences. Just try to keep writing until the timer goes off.

Optional part two: If you are working with a partner on these exercises, you can make a decision to share your writing by reading it out loud.

This is a powerful exercise that brings life to your words and thoughts. I would encourage you to honor one rule in this instance: no commentary. Just read and listen with an open heart. Both the reader and the listener, if aware, will be able to use the exercise and receive it as a gift.

In the woods, your compass tells you which direction you need to move in to reach your destination. If you ignore it, you might wander around aimlessly and end up going in circles. On the journey of life, fear plays the same role. If you ignore it, you might never get to where you want to go. But if you pay attention to it, you can use it as an indicator of what you need to work on so you can get to your destination: power, purpose, self-fulfillment and joy!

I'm not talking about survival fear here, by the way. We all have a hard-wired system that keeps us physically safe. Rather, I want to talk about the kind of fear that constantly sabotages our big desires, dreams and goals. The kind we already know we need to transform. The kind pushing us back into our comfort zone.

Using the deeper levels of awareness you've practiced in the prior chapters, you can begin to recognize when you're feeling fear. Once you recognize it, you have a couple choices: you can just think about it and end up doing nothing (thinking too much can be a paralyzing force), or you can view it as a sign that you need to take action. Taking action will empower you and provide you with a spike of courage that'll help you overcome that fear on a regular basis.

The solution to your fear, therefore, lies in taking action.

Take a moment to really let that soak in. If you can get your body to move toward your goal, in any small way, your fear will transform itself.

I didn't get brave overnight, and I'm not fearless. Through years of healing work, I learned a lot of secrets that helped me understand what's going on in my mind when I'm afraid. One of these secrets was that much of the way I was reacting to the events of my life had to do with things I'd experienced in my childhood, a time when I had to rely on other people for protection and nurturing. I learned certain people are safe, and others aren't. I learned to ignore my intuition when someone was being unkind. I learned the difference between conditional and unconditional love. I learned that creative freedom is dangerous. I learned I had to be a perfect, good girl to be worthy and safe.

For me, the hardest part about being brave was overcoming the core fear of being unworthy. Being thought of as "not good enough" created an instantaneous feeling of being small, weak, powerless and vulnerable, like a little three-year-old girl. My inner three-year-old couldn't stick up for herself or voice her opinions. She was afraid of being wrong or, worse, being punished. When that three-year-old was triggered, my fear wasn't rational: it was visceral, an automatic reaction to ensure survival.

In knowing I was meant for great things but simultaneously feeling I wasn't good enough, I began to feel an ache sabotaging my ability to feel joy. As a result, a fire started in my soul and burned until I paid attention and started to deal with it. That's code for: I started having chest pains.

To get beyond fear, I had to stand up inside my painful feelings and focus on present moment sensations, on my safe surroundings, so the feelings could move through me and I could heal. It wasn't easy; I had to practice over and over. I'm still practicing! It takes fierce discipline of awareness and courage.

In the end, fear, chaos, pain and turmoil became my greatest teachers. My journey of true healing began when I felt through those things and took action despite them. When I chose better, healthier, more aligned thoughts, beliefs and actions.

I learned that being brave meant feeling vulnerable and still doing or saying what I needed to do or say. Writing and publishing my first book made me feel vulnerable, but doing so made me feel more brave and sure about who I was and what I stood for. I shared my stories because expressing my truth was the best form of courage I could think of. Getting over my fear and sharing my stuff in the hopes of helping someone was what kept me going and keeps me brave today.

To free myself, I chose to take on a warrior spirit and let it be the way

I move through my world. I chose to transform my fears and play big. Every time I made the decision to be brave and forced myself to take risks, I sometimes made mistakes and sometimes failed, but I also guaranteed myself an adventure. Whenever I did it, I created miracles.

Following My Own Rules

The more I use my fear as a compass, the more readily I can do it. For instance, in one recent situation, a well-meaning colleague told me over Facebook chat, "You know, you should be careful about being too vulnerable in the groups you're trying to lead. People might not see you as a leader that way."

I wonder if she's right, I thought. My first reaction was to feel a pit in my stomach and realize it was the feeling of fear: the fear of being wrong. The reaction was defensive (fear-based), and I thought of sending her Brené Brown's TED talk about vulnerability. Why? To prove to her that I was right! But then I stopped for a moment, sat with that constructive criticism, felt the feelings it triggered in me, and let my body make a decision about what to do.

I realized I had nothing to prove; being vulnerable when I lead groups is what's right for me. Being open about my life is my lifeline, my oxygen. If I pretended or held back, I wouldn't be the kind of leader I want to be. I wouldn't thrive; I would suffocate. But I didn't need to communicate all this to her, I only needed to reaffirm it for myself.

So instead of reacting defensively by sending the TED link, I chose simply to acknowledge her comment. It was okay for me to hear her opinion because I recognized it as unique to her and the filters she was looking through. I didn't have to take it personally. This made the pit in my stomach go away.

I had allowed fear to be my compass once again and in that situation, experiencing my fear helped strengthen my resolve to believe in myself and my choices. I was reminded that the only person I ever had to answer to was myself. Nobody else could feel what I feel or know what was good or right for me. Aside from a few good mentors who were really only acting as mirrors, my greatest teacher sat in a place deep inside me.

Moving through fear means I can stand for something no matter what my critics say. It means I can be vulnerable inside of my truth and lead from that place. I can use courage to help me surf the waves of self-doubt and shame and learn not to judge others or take their opinions personally.

Messages from my Body

Carl Jung said, "What you resist persists." Until a few years ago, I was living that example, doing everything I could think of to convince myself what I was feeling—the tightness in my chest, the shortness of breath—was not a big enough deal to matter. But here's the thing: your body has a funny way of making you really uncomfortable when you're not listening to important messages. It forces us to be brave sometimes. Either we get fed up enough emotionally with our old conditioned behavior to change it, or the body lets us know we're not on track by making us physically uncomfortable and we have the choice of either remaining uncomfortable, or changing. Many people spend a lifetime without this understanding and suffer greatly in their search for a fix or cure.

My physical discomfort persisted for weeks and weeks. *Oh my God, I'm going to end up having a heart attack*, I thought. Finally, the daily, unrelenting chest pain was enough to kick me in the ass and force me to be brave and make some changes.

First, I had to figure out when and why I was feeling the pain. In the course of my healing work—my workshops, my journaling—I became more observant about my body and took note of when I was having a physical reaction to something. I noticed in situations where I stuffed down my own opinion, where I followed someone else's rules, where I was quiet and good, I felt physical tightness. This clued me in to the fact I that had some work to do: I had to deal with the fear of being myself and expressing myself to others.

I started expressing myself more than I ever had before, whether it was responding to a Facebook friend who didn't agree with something I'd written, reacting to a stranger who outright told me I was wrong, or reciting a poem to a room of 200 people. Each time, a tiny amount of healing occurred. I found courage in the act of saying things out loud (instead of in my head, as was my habit). It's how I was able to sort out who I am, what I'm worth, and what I stand for. These were my greatest victories over fear.

Empowered by these victories, I started expressing myself more and more: I wrote my first book, started blogging, began submitting my work to online publications, and asked people to read and listen to what I had to say. I was no longer afraid to talk about stuff that mattered to me; on the contrary, I was inspired to talk about those things. I got excited about engaging others in those important conversations. I realized I was put on this earth to go on the journey from feeling paralyzed to feeling powerful.

Mind you, all of this didn't happen overnight; I didn't suddenly find myself worthy and then go around telling everyone my opinion. I had to get brave first. I had to cannonball into expression with a slight inkling I'd be okay. I had to jump, risking sinking, but knowing sinking would bring me closer to knowing how to swim.

Coming from the Heart

In expressing myself more, one area I knew I needed to work on was my marriage. This was extremely difficult for me; the fear I felt every time I wanted to talk to my husband about something that bothered me mimicked the small and powerless feelings of the three-year-old again. I felt unworthy of stating my opinion when we were having a disagreement; I thought it would only upset him further. It was hard for me to get past the survival response that shut me down and sent me walking in the other direction.

But, little by little, I started talking to my husband about the ways I hurt and what was missing in our relationship. Somehow I would get the words out, saying things like, "Can you help me understand how you're feeling about the other night? It really hurt my feelings." I told him it was a struggle for me to be myself inside our marriage…that there was a battle being waged inside my own head. But I knew the only way to make a change was to get those thoughts out of my head. I had to take the action of expressing myself so he knew what was going on, rather than me stewing in resentment and waiting for something new to happen by itself.

Overall, I tried coming from what I call my "feeling space" and my heart, even though I risked him interpreting it as an attack. Every time I would open up to him, a small amount of pressure would release from my chest. It felt good.

If I'd listened to the messages my body was sending me sooner, I might've avoided some of the physical pain I experienced. But it took time and practice to learn the language of my inner warrior. I didn't always feel the messages or, when I did, I did a great job of ignoring them or numbing them out.

When someone was upset with me, I tended to retreat. I would hide, stay quiet, and not make waves. Confronting the problem head on was not my normal response. The problem with this scenario is it doesn't work for a marriage, or any important relationship. There are too many opportunities for others to make up their own meaning for your silence. Great, loving, effective communication requires you to speak up. The man I married became one of my greatest teachers as soon as I woke up to what he was helping me to do: become a better communicator.

I took away other lessons from my interaction with my husband also:
- If I allowed myself to feel the sensations without focusing on my "story" of whatever had happened, I could speak from a place of strength, as an adult warrior woman.

- I knew if I could remember to express myself from the place inside of me that feels instead of judges, I had a good chance of creating a discussion that heals instead of destroys.

Taking Action

Let's look at our reactions to fear. First, ask yourself these questions:

1. Are there any areas of your life where you need to be braver?
2. Are you feeling a tug inside you to pursue your passions, but ignoring it to focus on less scary endeavors?

3. Do you need to have an honest conversation with someone who matters to you but with whom you haven't been completely upfront about your wants and needs?
4. Are you avoiding making a hard decision that will affect others?

Whatever challenge you face, whatever is making you feel fearful—know the solution resides in taking action. Why? Because taking action will take you out of your head and give you the courage to keep moving forward.

At this point you may be thinking, *but what if I act and screw up?* It doesn't matter if you make a mistake or fail. Any kind of action taken ends up as a stepping stone on your path. You might as well lay down more stones and continue moving forward rather than stand on the edge of one, trying to decide which way to go all day long (consequently wasting days, months, even years of your life in the process).

If you dwell too long in your thoughts, analyzing and trying to figure out the "perfect" next step, you're staying in one place, paralyzed by fear. You're fighting a battle in your own mind. When you feel fear in your body, let it alert you to the opportunity to do the very thing you're afraid of. Begin to change the way you react to the feeling by thinking of it as something you can get excited about. When you feel the feeling, step back and observe it. Feel it without reacting. Lean into it just a bit.

As soon as you learn to escape from the box in your head that you've locked yourself into, you're free. When you begin to take the story out of the feeling of fear, fear becomes a sensation, like any other sensation in your body. Those sensations are there to be felt through.

Your action step can be any small thing: journaling, making a phone call, writing a goal list, researching a topic, asking for help, setting up a meeting. By doing something, you can unlock yourself from uncertainty.

You can also move your body. Physical movement is a great way to change the energy that keeps you stuck. Go for a walk, do some deep breathing, write a letter, dance, sing, shout, paint, clean out a closet… anything to move your body and boost your blood flow. The body's the door to the shift you want to make with your fear.

Peter Levine, the author of *Waking the Tiger: Healing Trauma*, talks about dealing with fear by going back to what you're feeling in your body. He says instead of forcing yourself to relive a past trauma, we should let our bodies remember by working with the sensations in the present moment. This allows trauma to move through you. The next step is to increase awareness by choosing a new way to think, believe, or act. Changing the "procedural" memory will allow us to break up the old patterns of fight/ flight or freezing and rehearse a different outcome.

Choose a new action, a new thought, a new behavior. Do something different in the face of fear and you'll change the story and create a new memory to go by or a new, healthy pattern to repeat.

There's power and magic in transforming fear. For the once-timid soul, this power and magic are miracles. We can work through the fear and pain keeping us from experiencing the joy we're meant to experience. It's possible. Anything's possible when you start to wake up and be brave. Anything you desire, anything you dream, can be realized.

If fear still has control over you and your life, stay open and curious about it. Continue to seek ways to heal and transform it. Know you may not have not found your way yet, but don't give up. In the next chapter, you'll learn about several possible healing modalities to use in addressing your fear. Each one is powerful and will resonate with people differently. It's worth exploring new techniques and different practitioners when you're looking for effective tools. Don't be afraid to try something new.

Know this: everyone's afraid. This isn't about becoming fearless. It's about learning how to be afraid and still function—shine, even—in your life. It's about learning how to use the energy of fear for you, rather than letting it work against you. Being fearless isn't the goal. Transforming fear into something that points you in the direction of your deepest desires is the goal.

It's the awareness and the courage that'll allow you to choose something new and different. Try it. What do you have to lose but fear?

7
Are You Hiding Something?

The Sound Of My Soul
by Laura Di Franco

I don't think you want
to hear my pain
I keep it inside
tucked away, forgotten.

It sits there
festering
and stuck
unavoidable.

I'm afraid to share
my darkness
I keep out the light
hide behind my big mask.

But soon it creeps out
black
and heavy.
The mask isn't big enough.

I'm terrified to be me
when I feel angry
I lock it up tight
hoping the clench will ease.

But it strangles
my heart

squashing my spirit
I have to speak.

Stepping into the pit
arms outstretched
to feel my way through
I hear something calling.

I follow
the sound of my soul
as it whispers
my name.
~~

The voice in your head says, "You're a bad girl. Shut up and do what you're told." And you believe it, so you stay quiet. You're ashamed to be you. Your past defines you. Your secrets rot inside your core and infect your life. Other people's reactions are proof that you've done something wrong, so you keep trying to make everyone happy by doing what they want and need and ignoring what you want and need.

Shame's another tricky, destructive feeling, kind of like guilt. There's no real benefit to feeling shame on the journey to joy. It's an old wound trying to exert its influence on you at a time far removed from the original event that created the feeling. Being ashamed to be yourself is its own shame, and maybe the only true shame that exists.

As women, shame about our bodies can be drilled into us from a young age.

"I can see your stuff," my aunt once said about my outfit on the first day of school. I had looked down at my just-budding chest and felt a hot flush fill my face as I nervously tugged my shirt up. I'd spend the next few decades wearing "appropriate" clothes, never revealing too much skin. I hid that way for a long time, feeling sickeningly self-conscious when I had to dress up or go out.

I spent a lot of time with my aunt; she was the cool one. She always had gum and extra cash in her purse, and she even shared pot brownies with me when my friends and I wanted to try them. When I could drive, I became her chauffeur and quickly realized her love was conditional. If I wanted things, I'd have to do what she said.

I remember being called a whore when she caught me sneaking my boyfriend into my grandparents' house, where I lived during a few college years. Even though I was old enough to make my own decisions, I still catered to her every whim. I learned I wasn't enough. That's how she held control over me for most my life.

What felt like nature taking its course—my sexuality and sensuality developing and expressing itself through my desire to have a relationship, including sex—was labeled bad. I learned I should be ashamed of myself. It would be a lot longer before that wound healed.

On Suppressing Myself

"Be quiet; we don't want to upset your father!" was something I heard often as a younger girl. I heard it constantly at my grandparents' house as well. Being too loud wasn't allowed, and if I broke those rules, I'd be shamed for it. Constantly being aware of the needs of everyone around me, to the point of behaving according to their rules and ignoring my gut in the process, became how I operated.

I also learned to suppress "inappropriate" emotions. Anger wasn't appropriate to express, according to my family, so I was never angry. Ruffling feathers meant I might be punished. If I got angry, especially at a family member, I was made to feel shame for it.

I never learned what intuition was. I never knew I had an internal guidance system that could tell me what was good or bad for me. And even if I instinctively knew about it, I was taught to ignore it and pay attention to what I was supposed to do, even if it went against my gut feeling.

Shame is another emotion that causes us to shrink inside ourselves. The funny thing about shame, according to most psychologists I've talked to, is that when you name it, it naturally dissolves. So, calling out shame by sharing the shameful thing with others is how you make the feeling go away. Keeping your shameful secrets locked inside is what perpetuates the suffocating feelings.

Another funny thing about the shameful stories I've shared is realizing that I'm never alone. What we think is shameful, what we think others will judge us or condemn us for, actually brings us all together. We connect with each other through our healing stories. We heal by telling them and by hearing them told by another. It's the exact thing we're afraid of that sets us free.

The shame I've held about doing drugs and drinking as a teenager and the desperate, needy way I lured men and used sex to feel worthy, well... that isn't me anymore. If I let those past events define me now, I'd be stuck in that prison until I died.

"When you know better, you do better."— Maya Angelou

I do better now. Much better. And when the old, familiar heat of shame fills my face today, I call it out as soon as I recognize the pattern. Shame has no place in a brave healer's life, except to teach her how to go for the joy. To give her awareness that'll change the world.

8
100 Ways to Call Out Shame and Fear

"No mud, no lotus."—Thich Nhat Hanh

One way to redefine healing is to begin to understand the different modalities available to you for shifting, healing and transforming pain, shame and fear. If we trash the idea that healing means being fixed and go for a much wider, more interesting, holistic and a little bit more magical definition, we get huge opportunities to explore, grow and evolve. I'd like to give you another way to think about healing (by feeling). Let's start with an exercise.

Warrior Exercise: It's Okay to Want More

Many of us are resigned to our lives the way they are, even if we're miserable. We're grateful for what we have and see that we don't have much to complain about. Don't get me wrong; gratitude is good. But most of us stop there and don't end up fulfilling our bigger mission and passion on the planet under the guise of resignation to playing much smaller than we could.

How do I know you have a mission? Because we all do. It's okay to want more than you have. This isn't greed we're talking about; it's desire. It's a core desire to enjoy more love and bliss. It's what you were born for. It's okay to want more of those things; in fact, feeling those desires is necessary if you want a life filled with more joy and health.

Feeling your desires is what inspires you. If you weren't meant to feel them, you wouldn't be inspired to do, say or create them. Start giving yourself permission to think about what you want. This can be more difficult than you think, but it's important to allow yourself to feel your deepest desires. Don't worry about what comes up; nothing you dream of in this moment is set in stone. You can always change your mind later. Danielle LaPorte has built an empire based on core desired feelings. When we focus on how we want to feel and imagine that feeling happening in our body and mind, we set ourselves up for manifesting that feeling. We get to leave the "how" it shows up to the Universe. It's the feeling that we're after, no matter what we choose to do with our lives.

You're meant to fulfill your deepest desires. It's time to start exploring what they are!

With that in mind, let's get into the exercise.

Take out your notebook, pen and timer. Set your timer for five minutes and fill in the blank: It's okay to want more for my life. One of my deepest desires is_____. Have fun with this. Don't censor yourself. Don't worry about spelling, punctuation or finishing sentences. Just write without stopping until the timer goes off.

Optional part two: If you are working with a partner on these exercises, you can make a decision to share your writing by reading it out loud. This is a powerful exercise that brings life to your words and thoughts. I would encourage you to honor one rule in this instance: no commentary. Just read and listen with an open heart. Both the reader and the listener, if aware, will be able to use the exercise and receive it as a gift.

Big Brave Question: Can I give myself permission to express my deepest desires?

Exploring the Mind/Body Connection

One of the hardest things to understand is that there's a psychological component to physical pain. So many patients have been told by a physician, "It's all in your head." And then they're shooed away with prescriptions for antidepressants or sleep aids. What if the doctor instead said something like, "I don't see any major physical cause for your pain. You have a huge opportunity to explore the connection to your mind. Here are some resources." What if?

It's like I told one client: "Everything's connected. When you're sad or angry, those emotions have a physiological manifestation in your body." My client nods. She gets it. She doesn't have to be convinced. But when it comes to her own pain, she denies it. "Yeah, but what's your diagnosis?" She wants a label. She wants to call it tennis elbow or give it some other easily fixable identification that gives her an ability to hand off the responsibility of fixing it to someone else. And that's when people like her give all their power away.

I've come to make asking questions about stress a common practice with clients. Not one person has wondered why I'm asking. They know it matters, because they can feel it in their bodies. Sadness, depression, anger, fear, doubt, shame and unworthiness all have physical feelings associated with them. Now it's time to link those feelings to your body parts.

When we begin to understand what we really have to heal, it can be both overwhelming and the best news ever. When the doctor says they can't find the source of your pain, be happy. Let your understanding of the mind/body connection give you hope. The physical symptoms can be coming from emotional or psychological issues. It's time to address all of you. It's time to embark on a healing journey that integrates mind, body and soul.

The reason this feels scary is because most of us know we carry plenty of mental, emotional and psychological baggage. It's heavy. We look at it and procrastinate, imagining that it's too hard, too painful, or just not worth the effort it'll take to change. We come up with excuses like: "Nobody can help me," "I can live this way," or "I'll never get better from this." The guilt, shame and fear we've locked down inside keeps us from starting the journey, and the old thoughts and beliefs keep us in a vicious cycle. We hang onto core negative beliefs about ourselves that sabotage our own happiness, health and healing.

Reaching out to get help is a bold move. There're many amazing paths to this kind of integration and healing. I've dabbled with many of them and will highly recommend seven you may want to try. Each path works by healing you as a whole. If one part is ignored, expect temporary or limited results.

Warrior Secrets: Seven Modalities to Start Your Healing Journey

The following seven healing modalities are by far not the only available options. They're the ones I've tried, loved and have gotten to work for me. They are here to get you thinking, hopeful, excited and interested in your own healing journey.

You never know where one interaction will lead you. Remember, the trick is to take action on what feels good. To use your intuition to follow the sacred bread crumbs. Here are seven paths you might explore. See what resonates and leave the rest.

Secret One: Emotional Freedom Technique (EFT)

One of the secrets I learned about current-day triggers, especially the likes of shame, guilt and fear, is that they're linked to events from long ago that challenged or shattered my self-worth. When I first learned the word "trigger," I assumed I was doomed to be triggered forever, that those weird psychological bonds could never be broken. I was wrong. There's a simple and powerful tool that can help to break up the trigger pattern, even if it's from an event in your childhood—it's called Emotional Freedom Technique (EFT).

Now that I know about this method, I love the name even more. It basically says it all, as the technique is used to recover your emotional freedom whenever something happens or someone says something that triggers an old feeling of fear, shame, unworthiness, humiliation, etc. The technique helps to break up the neurological link, so when the trigger happens, you don't feel the associated feeling at all anymore or don't feel as attached to it.

It essentially releases an old belief into the ether. As a result, you don't have to be doomed with the paralyzing force of that event anymore. After the event in my kinesiology class, it was a really long time before I spoke up or tried to do anything I thought was right or good. I was afraid to make a mistake and be humiliated again. EFT has helped break the link of the old memory to current situations that bring up similar fears. Now, I can make the choice to respond because I'm not locked in fear mode anymore.

In my first EFT session with a woman named Mary Phelan, I experienced crazy, amazing results. She started by asking me questions about what I was having issues with (current day) and then began digging deeper into my childhood moments, while linking them to my current issue.

Then we started tapping (the actual physical technique that breaks up the patterns). She would start by saying a sentence and tapping on a point on her face, and I would repeat the sentence and mimic her tapping on my own face. She would say the next sentence and tap on the next spot, and I would follow. Every round of tapping would end with, "And I love and accept myself."

I left feeling different, lighter, more positive and less "attached" to the problem I came in with. So far, the results have stuck. Every time I meet with her, something else breaks loose and more miracles begin to happen in my relationships. Every time I leave, I love and accept myself more and feel braver about being me.

One of my favorite online EFT teachers is Nick Ortner. You can find him and his books at www.thetappingsolution.com

Secret Two: Acupuncture

I found another secret in the ancient healing art of acupuncture. By releasing the blocks that were stopping up my energy flow, I experienced a unique form of healing. By now, you know we (as in our whole body, mind and spirit) are energy and vibration. Down to every last cell. When you get a chance to read more about this topic, make sure to pick up Bruce Lipton's book, *Wisdom of the Cells.* Because ancient cultures know that disease is caused by things that block up your natural energy flow, they treat the whole system, not just what hurts.

I met Robin many years ago after pulling her business card off the bulletin board of a local health food store. I was looking for someone in the area to treat my husband and his sinus problems. I ended up seeing her too and then continued seeing her for over a decade…eventually using her name when I had to fill out a form asking for my primary physician's name.

During our first meeting we sat across from each other in a tiny, naturally-lit, neutrally-colored, totally Feng Shui'd room and chatted about my fatigue and crappy immune system. "I catch every cold known to man," I told her. "Since my daughter was born, I can't seem to feel well. I catch like eight colds a year! I'm always exhausted."

She looked at me and said, "Well, I'm different than most healers." As a healer, I woke up a little bit in my chair and envied her confidence. At the time, I wondered what she meant, but after working with her a while I understood. And hoped I would get close in my own healing practice, even a tiny smidge, to the kind of healer she is. I knew she'd teach me new things about healing.

I never questioned her treatments and was always amazed at the way she tied our conversations to the needle points, smiling at the way I got stronger, healthier and less fearful. I trusted her to take me where I needed to go on my healing journey and followed along, practicing awareness in my body and my thoughts, until one day I felt like I had turned a corner and the momentum I had was self-sustaining.

Before then, throughout my treatment, I never asked when it would be "complete," and Robin never offered either. Because the reality is that if you walk into a healer's office, ask how long it will take to feel better, and hear them say, "three to five years," what would you think? You might feel overwhelmed. You may even throw in the towel long before your healing has had a chance to begin.

As I lived my life, with Robin to guide my process, the layers peeled away and I slowly (and in perfect timing) came into my radiant self, found my worth, began standing up for myself and my life, and changed my course. Acupuncture's one of the things that helped me get my flow back and heal every area of my life.

I remember a session where I was lying face down with the needles in my back. Robin had left the room and I was relaxing, trying to get into that zone that feels like half-sleep, half-daydream, an altered state of consciousness called the hypnogogic state. All of a sudden, I experienced a feeling of being very small, and I was terrified. I knew who and where I was, yet it seemed something was happening—a memory, maybe—that made me feel different. I let the tears come and used my awareness to allow the energy of whatever I was feeling to flow through me.

I knew it was fear. The combination of awareness and the reality of what was happening was, I would later learn, the key to healing things I never knew could be healed. I had to let the memory come up, allow myself to feel the fear as if it was happening to me in this moment, but at the same time stay aware of my surroundings as a passive observer of it all, to know I was safe.

It was—and is—amazingly effective. I still use acupuncture when something within me feels stuck or stagnant, if there's physical pain that won't go away, or if I need an immune system boost. I also use it for times I feel stuck in emotion, unable to pull myself out of the pit. I understand enough about energy flow now to know that acupuncture unblocks the flow.

You may be wondering what gets us blocked up in the first place, and the answer is, a ton of things, from emotional to physical to spiritual troubles. Illness, disease and pain are all signs of blockage, according to this Eastern philosophy of medicine.

When healing happens, sometimes it catches you by surprise, disguised as the release of pain or fear. I've come to know this as a healing crisis or therapeutic pain, and now I know what to do when I'm in one. When I bring my fully awake self to the experience, there's always a feeling of lightness, release and healing afterward.

Secret Three: Martial Arts (or Therapeutic Movement)

Another secret to healing came to me with the martial art of Tae Kwon Do. Over the years, as I slowly learned our tenants—courtesy, integrity, perseverance, self-control and indomitable spirit—I learned a discipline that would end up shaping the way I lived my life.

It all started when I watched a class one day with my then-five-year-old son to see if he wanted to try it. "What do you think, buddy?" I had looked down at him, rubbing his head affectionately.

"I'll do it if you do it," he had replied. It had begun as a way to connect with my son, but I found myself weirdly addicted to the new sport.

I still continue now, almost twelve years later—long after my son decided to move on to baseball—because the practice has given me more gifts of healing than I ever imagined it would.

Before Tae Kwon Do, I used to tell people that running was my meditation, that I used exercise to get still and focus on my life. After learning and practicing Tae Kwon Do, a mind, body, and spirit practice, I realized what I was doing during my runs was nowhere close to meditating or being still. In fact, it was the opposite of still. I used it to distract myself, to numb up.

Having grown up an athlete, when I started Tae Kwon Do I was in fair shape. Soccer from elementary school through sophomore year in college, followed by marathon training, prepared my legs for the martial arts, but what I didn't expect and quite obviously was lacking until then was the healing discipline it provided.

Tae Kwon Do forced me into the only place I could heal from: my body. While running, especially during hours-long training runs, I moved quickly out of my body and into my mind, where I'd hash and re-hash my worries, problems and fears. The repetitive and rhythmical nature of the run never demanded much focus. This new sport of Tae Kwon Do wouldn't allow me to zone out like that. If I wasn't present and paying attention, I was in trouble.

I remember my very first tournament and competitive sparring match as a blue belt, listening to the commands shouted out: "Charyut!" (attention stance); "Kyungnet!" (bow); "Joon Bi!" (ready stance); "Sijak!" (begin).

The adrenaline was doing a number on me. I stood bouncing on the balls of my feet, fists up, feeling somewhat paralyzed. I remember my first few kicks feeling weak. I could hear the sounds of the people and referees all around me echoing in my ears. The rules allowed full but light head contact for my division (the over forty adult blue belts). Oh my God, what am I doing, I thought, trying to avoid my taller opponent's kicks.

And then, bam! The kick to the right side of my head was so hard it knocked me over. I had to put my arms and hands to my sides, thinking I was going to hit the ground. I remember thinking, that was light head contact? Followed quickly by worries that I was in the wrong place. I heard my coach scream at the referee to stop the match. My opponent got a warning. The second kick to my jaw brought tears to my eyes. I can't do this, I thought. But I fought until the timer went off.

I was so unprepared that day. I was unprepared for the physical match, the emotions, the adrenaline rush and the humiliation of looking like a fool. I was unprepared for getting slammed in the head, twice. I blamed my instructors afterward for not training me appropriately. I had a hard time being aware of my surroundings, staying in control of my body and reacting well to my opponent. All things I thought I should have been taught by now.

Turns out I had some practicing to do. And it wasn't kicking I needed to practice.

The first gift I received from practicing Tae Kwon Do was a new definition of being aware. The secret is that there's a level of awareness you can achieve that'll take you further. I began to understand that I'd used running to numb myself out rather than feel. In Tae Kwon Do, I was forced to discover my fears and face them. I was asked to come up against the wall of fire and make a decision whether or not to jump through.

Over and over again, my moments of practice in the dojang and in the tests and competitions I've participated in have supported my healing journey. Another gift I received was joining a second family of sorts. The group of people I train with are outstanding. They're the reason I go. It's one thing to be a warrior on this journey but it's another entirely different thing to have a team of warriors on your side. When we're training together I feel I'm the best person I can be. They make me so.

A part of belonging to the school where I train is the opportunity to be tested for a promotion in rank. Yet another gift: the chance to see what I'm made of, mentally and physically. There's never a test that goes by where I'm not immensely grateful for my body and what it allows me to do. Not only do I advance in rank, but I'm given a chance to learn, grow and evolve as a student and teacher among my colleagues there. My experiences are automatically paid forward to the students below me when I get to teach them a new move.

The practice of Tae Kwon Do parallels the healing journey of life on many levels. When practiced with awareness, one has every opportunity to excel and move forward. Without that kind of focus, the practice becomes just another form of exercise.

Sometimes our lives become just another exercise: something we're caught up in but mostly asleep to. Does your life encourage learning, growth and evolution? Or are you floating along being jostled by the tide? It's up to you. The secret is awareness.

One of the biggest lessons I've learned from being an athlete is that I'm drawn to using physical performance as a way to identify myself. I spent twenty years defining myself by what I could accomplish physically, and it took a long time—and a few injuries—to wake up to who I was underneath that.

I encourage you to find the place for healing that works for you. Combat sports aren't for everyone, but the movement arts that train mind, body and soul are. There are many to choose from, including (but not limited to): yoga, Pilates, Feldenkrais, Alexander Technique, Nia Dance, Tai Chi, Qigong, Gyrotonic® Method, and Barre workouts. Not only will a movement arts practice and discipline be good for your body, but the family you create will be priceless. Every moment spent in a setting that nourishes your whole being is a little moment of healing.

I believe any form of healing occurs because, in that moment, you meet yourself as a divine being. You find yourself, as they like to say. I found myself many times over the years, when I was benched due to illness or injury, trying to figure out who I was if I couldn't do the thing I loved to do.

"You are God," motivational speaker Dr. Wayne Dyer said at the end of an inspirational talk I saw him give. "That divine spark is in you." I listened to those words, hung on them, and decided he must be right. And if he was, it meant however I defined myself prior to that very moment was slightly off. I wasn't any of the things I said I was: daughter, mother, sister, physical therapist, wife, athlete, friend. I was more than that.

Taking that in and knowing exactly what I was meant to do with it took many more years. I've learned that timing is all divine as well. I've learned not to bother with being worried about time.

So, the secret with using healing movement or martial arts comes back to how you spend your moments awake and alive inside of the practice and what you take from those moments to help you learn, grow and evolve. The next secret I'll talk about takes it all to another level.

Secret Four: John F. Barnes Myofascial Release

Secret number four is John F. Barnes Myofascial Release (JFBMFR). No book on healing should exclude this mind, body, soul technique. The founder, John F. Barnes, has been working hard to spread his message of love and healing all over the world, and we're finally in a time where people are paying attention. Not because of the science (although the research is coming) but because of the results.

I started learning his techniques early in my career, and as I used them, I watched my clients' pains disappear. The more I studied, practiced and got treated myself, the more I knew his way was the way I wanted to practice. Finally, a system of diagnosis and treatment that addresses the whole individual. Finally, a technique easy enough to teach the clients to do themselves. Finally, a way to live, in awareness, that positively affected the health and well-being of my clients and myself, both physically and mentally. Finally, a practice that would nourish me instead of drain me!

The biggest "secret" of JFB Myofascial Release is understanding the tissue itself. What we're taught in physical therapy school is grossly lacking. Now I understand the body/mind system is a miraculous combination of light and energy, with a communication system far more advanced than we thought. By addressing the fascia, we have the doorway to true, deep, authentic healing…an answer to injury, trauma and disease.

For those who don't know, the fascia is the three-dimensional web of connective tissue that makes up, surrounds and supports all of our internal structures. In its healthy state, it's fluid and carries light, energy and information to all parts of your body. When it's unhealthy due to inflammation, injury, or trauma, the tissue becomes dehydrated and restricted. Restrictions in the fascial web can cause huge amounts of crushing pressure on pain-sensitive structures in the body.

Restrictions are addressed with the technique of Myofascial Release. This's a combination of pressure and stretch applied to the body for several minutes (usually a minimum of five minutes in one area). The pressure and stretch stimulate something called the piezoelectric effect in the body which causes the fascia to begin to elongate and release, regaining its fluid, healthy state.

John F. Barnes Myofascial Release is performed through different techniques, including structural work, myofascial rebounding and myofascial unwinding. By addressing the person as a whole mind, body, spirit system, the techniques work to release the effects of inflammation, trauma and injury, including restriction, tightness and pain caused by stuck emotional energy.

The "release" of Myofascial Release can be both physical and emotional, and most of the time is both, as every injury or insult we incur is a combination of physical and emotional trauma. John has helped our Western medical system begin to integrate mind, body and spirit by teaching us how the fascial system operates. The newest research is confirming what we practitioners have known for over forty years: that everything is connected!

This was especially true for me one day as I laid face down on the treatment table during an MFR class. The hands-on stretch we were practicing didn't hurt, but the location of the stretch was bringing up a fiercely intense childhood memory of sea sickness. I had learned to let go, release and surrender to my fear by giving myself permission to feel. So I did. "I feel sick," I said to my partner, and then curled up into a ball, got really quiet and couldn't speak.

It brought me back to those weekends on my dad's sailboat after my parents' divorce when I would move between the bow of the boat and the cabin below, desperate for a place that would ease my motion sickness. Complaining wasn't effective, so I would curl up into as small of a ball as I could, keep quiet and try not to throw up.

That day on the MFR table I realized that healing doesn't always correspond with a physical injury. Healing is bigger than that. Healing accesses the parts of you affected by emotional, physical, or mental trauma; things that threaten your sense of being and worth in the world; and things that threaten your survival or put you into a fear state.

JFB Myofascial Release teaches the tools to access this stored, pent-up emotion and energy and allow it to be released from our physical tissues.

The work we did that day was part hands-on and part hands-off. How does the hands-off stuff work? It's all about energy. Everything is vibrating energy. We can vibrate at higher or lower frequencies. Energies at certain vibrations attract energies of similar vibration. When we think love, we emit that vibration. Love is what happens when we focus our intention on healing energy. When healing occurs with Myofascial Release, or any other form or technique, it's because love energy is present, and both client and practitioner are awake.

When you combine love energy with the hands-on release of tissue that holds old traumatic energy, you have a combination that can feel magical and results in authentic healing.

For more about John F. Barnes Myofascial Release, please visit www.MyofascialRelease.com
The next warrior secret I'll share is when you use this same awareness to move stuck energy from inside to outside through intuitive or therapeutic writing.

Secret Five: Therapeutic Writing

Writing can be a healing practice. My first writing retreat, Laura Munson's Haven writing retreat, showed me that when you find the thing you love more than yourself, you have a speed-dial to bliss. What would you do no matter if you were paid or not? If you don't know, therapeutic writing can help you find it.

When Laura began showing us the way to use writing to find our voice, I instantly knew I had found my thing. I wonder what would happen if I stayed here forever, I fantasized. I could find a little place, open up a healing studio, and write my days away. I wanted this so badly that I went slightly crazy with the idea of going home to my normal life. Laura called that "re-entry" and I began to understand why.

Bliss is a powerful drug—you'll do anything to feel it. When you know the difference between a normal life and one that creates bliss, you can't go back to normal. I went to Montana thinking maybe I could write, and I left knowing I could. The next months would prove it. My voice came alive on the page in the following days, and months and I gained clarity about my life's purpose by experiencing how good I felt when I was writing.

Writing and then sharing my voice out loud during the five days of that retreat was a healing experience I hadn't had before—a way to call out the doubt, shame, guilt and fear and give it all a witness.

I gave myself permission to feel the joy that the retreat unleashed in me. I started writing and submitting pieces like a madwoman, unattached to the outcome because for once, I liked what I was writing and didn't care what anyone else thought. For once, it sounded like me!

With every single blog and article that was published, I felt a little lighter. Long-pent-up secrets, opinions, emotions, and ideas poured onto the pages and were met with readers' "me too's!"

The secret of using writing as a healing practice is in how you let your soul speak on the page, how you are brave there. It's how you allow the world to know what is unknown. The simple act of writing your stories becomes a powerful awareness and healing tool. You can read my article, "9 Great Reasons Everyone Should Write," on MindBodyGreen.com and see how writing in all its forms is good for the soul.

Since my days in Montana and leading up to the publishing of this book, all I've done is write. I landed articles in a dozen different online magazines, including a regular spot in many of those, and ran my first online writing challenge and course. I changed my website to reflect my passion and finally began growing my platform. Haven gave me the mojo, and I ran with it.

The healing that occurred by staying awake for the experiences in that room with the other brave women there was magical. I couldn't have asked for a better week, with a more kind or patient teacher, more encouraging fellow students, or a more exciting or transformational experience.

If you love to write, write. If you love it more than you love yourself, then don't let anyone tell you that you can't. If you want to get better at it, then go learn from a master. If it's your dream, then start making plans for the dream to come true.

Since not everyone writes to make a living, I want to touch on the importance of writing to heal. When I started my course, Writing as a Path to Healing, I knew the combination of body awareness and therapeutic writing was going to be powerful. I knew I had something when the five brave women who beta tested my program were writing to me with amazing breakthroughs. I wasn't surprised when they said their lives were changing because of it. I knew the power of what I was teaching.

The proof continues to come in as the students of my course continue to write in with their aha's and breakthroughs. Awareness and writing—while seemingly so simple—have a profound affect for people, allowing them to transform years-old patterns of fear, shame and pain.

The secret of writing is no real secret, it's just that nobody really taught it to us as a healing technique. I was lucky enough that journaling drew me in from a young age. I smile now at my books, filled to the brim with secrets, dreams, answers, goals and complaints. I see even way back then, I healed on those pages.

One of the missing pieces in my childhood was sharing the writing. Oh my God, sharing what I wrote in my journal? Gasp! Yes, the feeling of not only writing but then reading aloud, being out loud in the world is indescribably empowering. It takes the right teacher and the right group of people to make that process safe and amazing. What I got in Montana I desperately wanted to give to my students. And now I am.

So, if you get stuck in something, are resisting something, are hurting, in pain or feeling hopeless, sad, angry or depressed, begin to Feng Shui your soul by taking out your notebook and writing that stuff from the inside to let it out. Make space in there. Clear it all out. You'll see that this simple act of writing is an amazing tool that you'll be able to use for a lifetime.

If you're interested in diving deeper, you'll find my online course, Writing as a Path to Healing on www.BraveHealer.com Many of the exercises in this book are there for you to explore.

Secret Six: Breathing

"I feel tingling," I said, looking up at Lauren with worry.

"It's okay, keep going," she encouraged.

"My hands are cramping up," I said to her with growing concern.

"It's fear coming up," she said confidently. "It's okay, let it come," she nudged. And I breathed, deeply and steadily, for many more breaths, feeling the tingling and cramping and allowing tears to come.

We sat in a large bedroom in her home, on the floor, leaning against yoga chairs. The mat next to us in the center of the room, covered in comfy-looking pillows, was where I'd end up. I noticed the music speaker and the huge white crystal singing bowl on the shelf behind her. Something's happening, I thought. At the same time, I was strangely not afraid of hyperventilating or passing out (and never did). I was ready for whatever this was.

What I was experiencing was the sixth, and greatly profound, healing modality I'd like to recommend to you: transformational breathwork.

Yes, breathing. Seems like a no-brainer, right? Breathing's important. We can last about seven days without food. We can last a few days without water. But we can only last a few minutes without breathing. Breathing's our life force.

When I was introduced to breathwork, I went in as I usually do when trying out a new healing modality: excited and open to possibilities. It was hard for me to fathom breathing for an hour and a half (the session length), but I trusted my teacher, Lauren, and was ready for the adventure.

Through a similar combination of intuition, dialogue and technique (as all the prior mentioned modalities use), I was thrown into a profound experience I'd never felt before. The power of my deep, connected breaths began to wash me out. It felt like an energy buzzing in my body and moving into the crevices where my shit was hiding.

I experienced both physical and emotional release during the session and left wondering what the fuck had happened. I also left with the sense I'd just stumbled upon one of the most powerful healing tools that exists, and it was here for the taking all along. I have used breathwork in some form or another every day since that first session.

So, when in doubt, breathe more. Find a local breathwork practitioner and learn more about the technique. There are many different ways breathing is taught, and no one way is the right way. Try different techniques and see what works for you.

For more information, go to Lauren's website: www.ExperienceBreath.com

Secret Seven: Coaching

Shortly before the writing retreat, I met secret number seven - a coach named Torrie. Like lots of miracles that've arrived over the years, I found her on Facebook, in a group I was part of.

Something I know now that I wish I knew then is we're not here to do this alone. The love, support, assistance and wisdom of a good coach is priceless. I soon found that out after hiring Torrie.

After starting to work with her, the first time I'd ever jumped into the world of coaching other than sports, I wondered why I'd never thought about bringing a helper into my life before. Things were about to get interesting in ways I'd only dreamed about prior to this. "The vision I have for you is really, really big," she would say to me during our first couple sessions. And I believed her.

The inspiration and motivation I felt after letting Torrie be that outside observer, that extra special pair of eyes and ears with perspective I hadn't learned to gain on my own yet, was kick-ass; truly life-changing. She would go on to teach me the superpower of my own intuition and give me a gift of a lifetime.

"When you're serious, determined, positive and on-purpose, magical shit happens."—Torrie Pattillo

This kind of inspiration shifts your energy. I'm addicted to it now. And since one of the biggest secrets of life—Inspiration + Action = Results— was my default setting, I started manifesting things. My writing began to gain traction online for the first time ever. Ideas began showing up in my mind. With Torrie's help, I started to figure out what my real purpose and mission on the planet was.

She helped me understand the language of my intuition. This has become a priceless tool that guides me daily, sometimes hourly. I started my career wondering about the lucky people who had intuition. I left Torrie every session knowing I possessed that power, feeling excited about developing it further.

Getting a coach allowed me to take a deep breath and be okay with not knowing all the answers. As I sat back and let her teach me, I felt a huge wave of momentum pick me up and carry me.

In case you didn't catch it, secret number seven is finding a teacher who cares about your success and helps you take everything you've done, healed and learned and fashion it into a life you can't wait to wake up to every morning.

The more I let go of my past and imagine my future as if it's already happened, the faster things appear. This requires me to keep feeling the feelings, be brave and choose beliefs and actions that serve my desires. Resistance dissolves in the middle of my awareness, my tears, and my vulnerability. I feel the healing inside of the practice, no matter which avenue I choose to bring that awareness.

No matter what path you choose for your own healing journey (because there're so many good ones) the actual secret to the healing is a combination of awareness and an ability for your practitioner or coach to hold a healing space for you. Both you and your coach have to practice a healing presence.

When this happens, energy can be moved, affected, and transformed. That's what I call healing. Mary, Robin, Master Holloway, John, Lauren and Torrie are all doing the same thing: moving energy. Find the way that works for you, whether it's tapping, acupuncture needles, a movement art, hands-on stretch, therapeutic dialogue, writing art, dancing, coaching or therapy, and jump in with two feet. Find your guide. Be brave. Start climbing the mountain.

Most healing adventures start with you feeling like you're standing at the base of what looks like Mount Everest. You're looking up wondering what the fuck you've done. You're excited but scared shitless. The voices in your head are so loud, you can't hear yourself talk. *This is a bad idea,* they say. *You might get hurt,* they remind you. *You are crazy to even think about this,* they go on. They're letting you know every possible reason you should quit, turn around and head for your comfort zone. They're reminding you of past failure, of what you should still be ashamed about. They're reminding you how much easier it will be to stay put on your cozy couch at home and watch the climbers on TV.

Are you awake? Are you hearing that inner critic? Do you realize that sitting on the couch will get you no closer to the summit? Be brave. Now's the time. Hear what's going on. Use your tool of awareness. Right now! And start climbing.

How Naming Your Inner Critic Can Silence Her Nagging Voice

I'm sitting in the little cottage at a meditation retreat last year. I'm surrounded by women who're here to heal, be brave and get closer to their truth. It's time for introductions and as soon as I hear that plan, my heart is thumping. I look down and wait for the lurching.

Why is saying my name so hard? Why can't I feel comfortable in my own skin? Why can't just being me bring joy instead of fear and dread? Instead of listening to the other amazing women introduce themselves, I'm consumed with self-consciousness and fear. I'm over-thinking my introduction, trying to come up with something important to say. Something I think they'll want to hear, something that'll make them like me. I fail to listen to what any of them are saying. I'm not here, present in my body, but trapped in my fearful mind and feeling the effects of that jail.

The weight of this story is heavy on my heart. I've lived my whole life feeling like this. Healing for me has meant letting go of the need to be liked or to fit into others' boxes. I've found the answer to letting go in all of the different ways I've described above. It came in small chunks some days and huge boulders on others.

This particular weekend, it comes in my ability to recognize the inner critic voice and name her, something Laura had taught me at Haven. This puts the voice at a safe distance outside of me. I finally hear the voice as separate from me and my intuition. After that weekend I began to practice putting myself out there. And I began to help others in that space as well.

"Okay, the first thing we'll do is go around and introduce ourselves." I'm watching the faces of my first group of writing workshop participants. "I'd like you to practice being present for this. Don't worry about what you're going to say. Listen to your fellow writers. I'm going to give you another chance to say anything you missed the first round!"

"That's a brilliant idea!" One of them said softly. I smiled. "Right?" I said. "So we can just relax, and we'll have a round two!" I repeated. Everyone seemed to relax and as the introductions continued, I remembered the day at my meditation retreat and noticed that my heart felt calm now. I was home.

One Final Secret to Being Brave

One last secret to knowing my worth, being brave and going after what I want has been to stay awake and keep looking. To not give up. To make the awareness of my awareness a daily goal. Always the seeker.

My breathworker reminds me often that fear is just excitement without the breath. If you think about being afraid, you'll notice that your breath becomes shallow, rapid. When we take the fearful sensations we're feeling—the same ones that usually paralyze us—and breathe with them, we can transform them. It's possible to do the thing you're afraid to do.

I'm pretty sure I was born to be brave, feel amazing and show others the way. It's nice to know my soul's mission. I'll end this chapter with a powerful dream I had.

Kneeling before Thich Naht Hahn (yes, the famous Buddhist author of Being Peace and one of the most well-known heart-centered guys on the planet), I thought in the dream, that's Tich Naht Hahn! (There was media coverage in real life that he'd been in the hospital, and I was feeling a strong desire to read them in detail, which is odd for me because I don't watch the news.) In the dream, there were a slew of onlookers lined up facing us, sitting cross-legged on the floor, similar to how we sit at the end of our Tae Kwon Do class, facing our instructor for a moment of stillness before the end of class.

Thich gave me a hug, demonstrating how if the hug was done one way, you would have one result and if it was done another way, you would have another. Grabbing him gently around the waist, I hugged back. My head turned and rested softly on the robe at his stomach. For a brief moment, I felt submissive; then, as I felt his arms around me, I melted into the feeling of complete acceptance. Yeah, this can save the world.

This feeling of complete acceptance was like none other. The dream was palpable, more than others I've had. I woke with heavy remnants of the feeling in me, and it's lasted without wavering as a knowing that I'm enough, I matter, and I'm worthy of the deepest love. Fear has had a way of fizzling out since that night. I feel there are many of us whose entire lifetimes have been a journey of reclaiming our worth, of feeling loved and accepted in the world. Some might have such a dream and think nothing of it. Someone who's aware, however, knows it's a message. And it's that knowing that can change everything.

In the next chapter, I'll talk more in depth about worthiness to help you understand you're born worthy, that it's not something you need to try to earn.

9
Are you Enough?

The Light Inside
by Laura Di Franco

Hiding inside
all my life
unaware of who I am.
It takes years
of heartfelt tears
to discover I can

be myself
shining bright
aware inside of now
pure joy to feel
loud, clear and real
I choose to see the wow

in life's gifts
challenges and lessons
a worthy journey they all make
it's such a relief to be
the best possible me
no matter which path I take

I realize I am
the light inside
the love, the joy, the grace
with courage found
and purpose sound
I'll heal the world today.

The voice in your head says, *you're not good enough or smart enough. Nobody wants to hear what you have to say. You don't have anything of value to add. You don't matter. You're not worthy of success, love or joy.*

You seek worth and validation through outside means, always doing the thing that'll make you feel right or perfect. Achievement is your drug of choice, and you like to get high. But nothing fills the hole in your soul until you begin to love yourself. Problem is, you've never been taught how to do that, or even what that looks like.

One day, my dad flat out told me his love for me was conditional. I felt I had to earn love by being a perfect, good girl, and I've spent most of my life believing that. I looked for it with many men before meeting my husband. I did everything I thought I needed to do to be loved and feel worthy. Everything, that is, except love myself.

I allowed myself to be treated poorly. In high school, I did drugs, drank and had sex with a lot of men to feel worthy. If I was with someone, it meant I was okay. If nobody wanted me, it meant I was shit. I had such low self-esteem and self-worth, I couldn't feel worthy without external validation or acknowledgement. And even with those, it wasn't easy. I've spent decades unlearning a core belief that I'm unworthy.

If there was no man in the picture, I went after achievement instead. I cringe when I think about the person I was; I feel sorry for her, but I've learned, through the art of self-compassion, to be gentle with myself. I've come a long way and ultimately had to come home to myself and my worthiness to heal. I practice some form of this every single day.

I've learned that nobody needs fixing; we're not broken. I've learned and believe it's more about peeling off the layers of dirt that cover up your light. I started feeling my light during profound healing experiences—Myofascial Release, Acupuncture, Breathwork, EFT, Tae Kwon Do—and started to understand what was meant by the saying "we don't need fixing."

Feeling worthy was a door to healing, and it had nothing to do with changing anything about who I was. It's been about finding, feeling, and expressing who I already am and then loving her with a wild fierceness, like I love my own children. It's about understanding my sacred desires and giving them a voice. It's about giving myself permission to be me.

Nobody else, despite all their praise, adoration and positive feedback, has been able to give me this gift. I had to find it on my own, allow myself to believe it, and then make it what I stood for. The positive people in my life have been key, but ultimately I had to come to a new belief on my own. Looking within for the answers, and learning the language of my soul, was how I reclaimed my worth, surrendered my past and began to live in the bliss of my now.

The Journey to Myself

The journey to passion and power has been a journey to myself, in all my ferocious goddess glory. Standing in my worthiness ended up being the key, and remains the constant challenge. It became possible when I woke up, started noticing how I felt and began listening to my intuition.

When you start to believe you've arrived at some enlightened end or spiritual nirvana, life has a funny way of showing you it's about the journey and not the destination. We have to get comfortable with feeling uncomfortable. We have to expect to be triggered into the next level of opportunity the day we believe we've arrived.

We can be grateful for the chance to peel off another layer, to free ourselves from the prison of unworthiness even more than we thought possible. This'll happen as soon as you realize your worth becomes something you're born with and not something you need to earn. As soon as confidence replaces doubt more often than not and we understand that our unique message is one someone else is waiting to hear, then we'll start to feel the kind of courage brave healers feel.

You know it deep down: you're enough. It's nice if someone else tells you, but it's time to tell yourself, and actually believe it this time. You can live out the rest of your life letting yourself be paralyzed by the past and its old grip, or you can spend the rest of your days practicing something new. Be brave. I'll show you how in the next chapter. In the meantime, remember that you have a choice, in every single moment, to take action based on your desires and with what aligns you with your dreams, or to stay stuck in old wounds. This is challenging work. But you're a warrior.

10
Standing Tall Inside Your Worthiness

"Self-worth comes from one thing: thinking you're worthy."
— Dr. Wayne Dyer

It has to end here, with worthiness. If you don't continue to use awareness to ultimately arrive at self-love and self-worth, none of this will last. Self-worth and self-love are the last and only solutions because they're what the brave healer spends her life fighting for. Once self-worth is rediscovered or reclaimed, it's about what you do to maintain, grow and evolve it to transform your life from where you are now to where you want to be. From a place of worth, confidence and authentic, unapologetic expression, we journey with passion and power and we change the world.

Let's do an exercise to help us get to that next level of awareness.

Warrior Exercise: Fierce Body Awareness

Have your notebook, pen and timer handy. Find a comfy place and relax. Sink down deep into your body. Melt and soften there, inside yourself. Let the sensations of your body be the dwelling place for your mind. As thoughts float in, watch them and release. Come back in. Bring your attention to the skin, to the breath, to the weight of your body on the chair or bed. What does it feel like today?

Notice your thoughts. What's happening as you scan your body for sensation? Breathe a bit deeper now and let your breath be the thing that anchors you into the moment. Feel every piece of the inhale and every piece of the exhale. Soften into the moment, and honor the stillness there. Be grateful for your body.

Begin to connect the inhale with the exhale. Start by breathing in through your mouth and out through your mouth. Let every exhale be a release, letting your body soften with each one. Take the next inhale before you are fully done with the exhale, connecting the breath so it becomes continuous. Notice how this makes you feel.

Watch your thoughts: stay in the sensations. Relax and release, letting go more with every exhale. Feel the energy in your body. Allow yourself to let go. What parts of your body do you notice as you breathe? What feelings or emotions do you notice in your body? You are experiencing everything through your awareness: what do you feel?

Soften your breathing and come back to the room and your surroundings. Notice any sensations as you bring your attention to the environment. When you are ready, grab your notebook and pen and set your timer for five minutes. Fill in the blank: When I really let go, I_____.

Remember: no rules, just write.

Optional part two: If you are working with a partner or group on these exercises, you can make a decision to share your writing by reading it out loud. This is a powerful exercise that brings life to your words and thoughts. I would encourage you to honor one rule in this instance: no commentary. Just read and listen with an open heart. Both the reader and the listener, if aware, will be able to use the exercise and receive it as a gift.

Big Brave Question: What is one way I can stay awake to the stuff of my life?

After becoming aware at the meditation retreat that my self-consciousness was causing unnecessary fear, I paused and realized that none of it mattered. We all mattered equally. We all mattered. And none of this fear and self-consciousness mattered. Worth is something I was born with, not something I need to try harder to earn. I could step forward with this new belief, this knowing, and align with my biggest desires, dreams and goals.

I don't remember how I finally introduced myself at the retreat. I fell back into the safety of my body and said the words and breathed and noticed the eyes of the women smiling around me, and in that moment, made a decision to know I mattered, no matter what I did for a living, what I achieved, (or not), or whether or not I succeeded at anything. I decided to matter no matter what, and in that very moment, I knew what I was meant to discover, learn, and teach.

If awareness is the key to healing, then love is the energy we wrap ourselves in to shift and transform our fears into what serves our greater purpose. Love is many things: forgiveness, letting go, compassion, empathy, kindness, awareness, and acceptance. First, we must be able to receive all of these things from ourselves. Only then can we expect to be able to give them to others.

Are you loving yourself these days? Remember, you're already worthy. There's nobody on the planet that'll say any magic words to make you more worthy than you already are. They may wake you up to it, though, so paying attention is key.

This chapter is about transforming fear, shame and humiliation (the tough stuff) into love. It's about going from powerless to powerful. From confused to confident. How does that happen? In an instant with awareness and forgiveness; when you realize you're worthy, the old triggers don't have a strangle-hold on your heart anymore. Using awareness to make the decision to walk away from what keeps you fearful and chained to the past is a form of self-love.

Warrior love is a special energy in which we bathe our awareness in. It's a kind of healing awareness. If we practice awareness only to judge and berate ourselves and others, it won't do the work of healing. You have to add love to awareness to get healing. You have to vibrate higher to feel it.

Warrior love will be how you forgive past hurts. It'll be how you navigate your relationships, and it might even be what we're all here on the planet to experience.

Using Narrative Therapy to Heal

I spent a full month a couple of Novembers ago doing the NaNoWriMo challenge (to write a 30,000-word book in thirty days). A memoir about my childhood had been moving it's way through me a couple weeks prior to finding out about the challenge, so I knew the timing was perfect. I titled my book, *Love in a Nightmare.*

The program served as the motivation I needed to let all the hurt, pain and memories move out of me onto the page. That book ended up being 65,000 words. I had a few stories to tell about that time of my life.

I had a sense of therapeutic writing before then from decades of journaling, but something happened when I let myself write the entire story without censoring. I was able to integrate the trauma sitting in my right-brain with my left-brain to give the feelings a story, and move them out of me. I was told by a psychologist that the name for this process is narrative therapy. I didn't care if it had a name. All I knew was that something good happened when I told the stories.

Sitting at my laptop in the early Christmas Eve morning, the year I finished *Love in a Nightmare*, I attached my memoir to an email and hit send. The book was now in my family's hands.

"You better not publish that!" My dad was the most hurt and defensive. Neither of my parents ended up finishing the book. Sharing those vulnerable feelings with my family started wreaking havoc in the lifelong patterns that were an ingrained dynamic amongst us. I triggered them, and probably myself, big time. Then I sat with the chaos that ensued and thought, *I wonder if any of this was worth it.* The warrior love I had to practice was about doing the thing I needed to do for healing; to prioritize that healing above the discomfort. To risk being bad in order to save myself.

"Daring to set boundaries is about having the courage to love ourselves even when we risk disappointing others."—Brené Brown

Even though it was painful for them to hear the stuff that'd been stuck in me for decades, it opened up a channel of communication that did not exist before. I began speaking up. They began listening and responding. My world changed. Forgiveness led the way, and I started to think maybe I could be myself and still be worthy of love. This was one of the biggest revelations ever, and I was definitely high on the fumes of shift.

Maybe my parents (and some teachers) weren't practicing awareness during my childhood. Their choices in parenting and teaching certainly reflected that in some moments. If I judge them for doing what they could with what they had from where they were, then I'm just as unconscious. Instead, I choose to be grateful for my life...even the more difficult moments. *Especially* the more difficult moments.

Soul Contracts and Forgiveness

"We make soul contracts. The people in your life agreed to be there. To do what they're doing on purpose to help you learn a lesson, grow or evolve. You both agreed to this arrangement." As I lounged on my down comforter, pink earbuds inserted, and listened to those words from Radical Forgiveness, I felt the acknowledgment of what I already knew: my dad's role in my life was to help me feel worthy—badass worthy.

Now, whether or not you believe in soul contracts, because I know I'm getting a little woo-woo here, just maybe this perspective could help. I've learned to ask, what else is possible? I've learned to ask big questions to keep my mind in curiosity instead of judgement.

Judgement's just a personal opinion based on the unique lenses a person's looking through. Those lenses could have been stained umpteen different colors based on the person's personal life experience. Maybe we could stop looking at judging others or situations as a bad thing and start understanding that we all judge everything, all day long. It's how we function, make decisions and survive. Maybe we could more easily stop taking others' opinions personally and start being able to communicate from a place of mutual respect...even when we disagree. Imagine.

I started realizing I'd been judging my parents and teachers as wrong or bad, and not understanding this deeper idea of the lenses I was looking through. I had some work to do. It's very possible my dad felt trapped in his life. No doubt he was living out the duty and obligation he felt. Maybe kids were never a huge desire of his. Maybe parenting wasn't something he felt he needed to practice or improve upon.

One of the biggest aha's of my life came recently after reading that book about forgiveness and it was about my dad. Everything in my life is totally okay, spiritually perfect. Including everything my dad has ever said or done. Nothing happened to me. Everything happened for me. *I get to sit here and write this book about healing because of my dad,* I thought as I sat furiously typing one day. *That passion is partly due to him!*

Another huge lesson sat inside of my urge to blame. Writing my stories of pain and blame woke me up, and I knew I was finally free. I still had to claim the memories, feel them and know the truth…but I didn't have to jump into the pit of quicksand of the past. Are you standing on the edge of that pit? Or are you knee-deep most days? Can you see every moment you spend in past pain and blame keeps you stuck? Forgiveness can get you out of that pit, but it isn't for anyone but you to claim.

Start using your awareness to realize when you're stuck in a thought about the past. That quicksand will suck you down faster than anything. Don't step in it. Catch it as soon as the thought enters your mind and shut it down. Move on to arriving in the present moment by taking a deep breath and sinking into your body to feel the feelings. Let them move through you, and try not to analyze too much. Breathe. Focus on something that feels better.

The thing about my stories was I realized I didn't want to be defined by them anymore. *I'm different now,* I thought. The past didn't fit in that bigger frame. I started really loving the "me" who was emerging, and it was harder and harder to want to think about the past I was writing about. *This isn't the book,* I thought one day, *my story is much bigger than this.* That was the day my story changed and I began the journey of writing this book.

Part of the transformation involved loving myself enough and the other part was being able to love my family no matter what happened in the past. If I felt different, surely they were also different. Likewise, if I wanted to be treated differently, then surely I would have to treat them differently. It would begin with my awareness, along with my ability to be brave in my conversations with them. It would happen by me being my new self and being unapologetic about that. It would be about setting boundaries for the first time in my life.

I would have to stand up for myself, not only with my family but with everyone I encountered. I would need to be brave about choices I made about who I spent my time with.

It was time to know I mattered and to go for my biggest desires and dreams.

I wrote my family a letter that week. Here's a piece of what I journaled about the experience: *"I am thinking the ties that have bound me to family all these years are changing. We stuck together out of survival...but I was always trying to fit into a role I never chose. My role has changed. I have changed. I can't be in the old box anymore."*

I grew up thinking being loved meant following the rules, behaving, not making a fuss, and keeping quiet. Now I know that sometimes the deepest love you can express comes from the courage to feel it for yourself first, before you try to give it to anyone else. I had learned that was selfish. Now I know it's necessary. This's another kind of tough love: when you risk not being liked to do the right thing for yourself.

Setting (and Keeping) Boundaries

I once had a long-time client who couldn't wake up. She numbed out on prescription drugs and had many excuses why she couldn't wean off them. I knew I wasn't going to be able to help her...yet I kept agreeing to schedule her sessions. One day, we had a scheduling issue and she blew up at me over the phone. My honest mistake was unforgivable, and she chose to call me names over it.

"I won't be able to see you anymore," I finally got the nerve to say, my body trembling.

"Oh, I'm going to keep seeing you," she said.

"No, it's time for you to find another practitioner," I said, staying brave, and ended the call abruptly so as to not continue to fight a battle neither of us would ever win.

Warrior love means doing the thing you know you need to do to keep yourself healthy and sane, no matter what happens. In the process, you force others to look at themselves and, in the best cases, to heal their own shit. When you imagine the worst possible scenario, remember that you have no idea what miracle you may be creating for the other person; you just assume the worst, but it could be the best thing that ever happened to them. Your boundary could be the thing that wakes them up for the first time ever.

If it's all about awareness, then it's also all about loving ourselves. This kind of love, Warrior Love, is about your fiercely alive whole self, and it has to be your priority. The only way to move through the fear, shame and humiliation of our past is to accept those parts of us completely, discover how to love ourselves, and use fear as a compass. Only then can we step into the warrior we should be.

And I don't mean kinda, sorta love ourselves. I mean for real. Like, with everything you got. Badass self-love. All the time. Forever. You have to be your own protector, supporter and cheerleader. If you happen to have others in your life who do that for you too, consider it icing. You don't have to do it alone, you just have to be intent on doing it no matter if you are alone or not.

This step is critical because the voices of our past will continue to try to sabotage. The self-aware, self-loved individual possesses special armor that stands up against this kind of attack.

The kind of attack that came one afternoon as I sat at my computer staring at the screen and felt a familiar pang in my chest. *Oh my God*, I thought. The email from a family member could have trashed every ounce of self-worth I had left. Rather than feeling the old, familiar chest squeeze and torturing myself with "bad girl" thoughts, I used awareness and the energy of love to transform the moment.

I had to think differently. I had to recognize my fear voice, separate it from myself, and realize it wasn't me. Then I had to decide how I was going to respond to the email, if responding was even an option.

OMG, I thought, *you're still stuck in the past; still letting fear run your life!* The aha in that moment was that I felt completely done with that shit. I took a giant pair of scissors (in my mind) and cut the cord chaining me to who I had been, to all the thoughts and stories wrapping me up in the old me. The idea of acting out of guilt, fear or obligation melted away.

That was the day my chest pain disappeared. The truth about healing is that it's complicated. It's a chaotic mess of tangled-up mind, body, and soul strings. Sorting out the threads isn't going to happen by forcing, or pulling tighter. You have to slow down, look at the big picture, and see where you can start untangling the knots. Most of the time, if you can get yourself to slow way down inside your feelings, you'll have a fighting chance to feel them, sort them out, and let them move through and heal. Most of us ignore, stuff or numb ourselves instead.

Fear's one of the important strings. I've learned that when I feel fear in my body, I can always count on it being something I need to pay attention to, as well as something that'll change the course of my life, if I'm willing to feel it, face it and take action.

That's the thing: feeling it sucks. It hurts. It's messy. It's vulnerable. It's terrifying. We'll do anything not to feel it. Avoidance and resistance are the norm when it comes to feeling fear, shame and humiliation. It's what we've been taught. The whole thing looks like this gigantic wall of fire; nobody's willing to jump through it. Instead, we get numb. We drink, do drugs, work a thousand hours, or do hot yoga until we can't move. Thing is, you can't selectively numb emotions, says Brené Brown. If you numb the fear, you also numb the joy.

Every time I've forced myself to jump through that wall of fire, I get to the other side, look back over my shoulder and think, *Shit, that was easier than I thought.* What happens is we don't see that the wall's just a millimeter thick, and we get paralyzed by its size and scariness. We stand there frozen and stare at the wall, or more likely, high-tail it in the other direction. We're feeling what our three-year-old self felt, when we were powerless to do anything. Only now, we're adults and we *can* do something!

I'm not talking about walking-down-a-dark-alley-at-night kind of fear. The flight-or-fight response in your body that occurs for survival is another sort of thing. I'm talking about the uncomfortable, tight, difficult, annoying, frustrating, desperate, aching feelings of fear that keep you from doing what you really want to do in your life and from being your magnificent, uncensored, unapologetic self. This's the fear that the brave healer fights every day.

Getting used to the presence of these feelings, recognizing them for what they are, and beginning to use them as a compass can be a total game-changer in the evolution of your goals, dreams and future.

Warrior Exercise: Fear as a Compass

Ready for a journaling exercise? Grab your notebook, pen and timer. Take a few breaths to clear your mind and connect with your breath and body. Set your timer for five minutes and write about the following scenario: If there were nobody left to offend, upset or disappoint, who would I become?

Big Brave Question: Ask yourself, what else is possible when it comes to moving through fear?

Instead of running in the other direction, what if we learned a new way to deal with fear? Instead of finding ways to numb ourselves to the feelings, what if we learned how to feel the feelings and choose another option? What if fear could be the way we know we're about to do something that will change our lives for the better? It would change everything!

"When you feel fear, you are bumping up against the walls of the small box you are in, and you are about to transform and move to a much bigger box."—Mary Phelan, EFT Practitioner

Changing the way we react to the feeling of fear may sound like a big leap, but it's a leap that will lead to your bliss.

In February of 2014, I boarded a plane bound for Quantum Leap, a class given by my Myofascial Release instructor, John F. Barnes. I sat alone in a row of three seats and had a moment I can only call divine intervention. Reaching down between my feet for my purse, I grabbed the notebook and pen tucked inside and began writing. Here's what came out:

God on the Plane

"The journey begins. The cab was early. The plane is on time. Everything was done, organized, arranged and confirmed. From Dulles to Dallas to Sedona, I am sitting by myself in a row of three seats. Yep. Little ol' me. Space. I'm filled with excitement and anticipation, as I've been feeling the energy of this event building in the last few weeks. From test achievement to depression to sad lunch to joyful birthday weekend in an unforgettable snow…don't think I don't feel you, Universe, that push that nudges me from behind, crowding my space, waiting for me to make a move. Instead I sit still in myself and feel it. I don't go to class. I don't fake the lunch. I listen and feel. And I recognize the okayness of the moment even in its dampness. That makes me breathe. And I don't get tighter. I feel and trust in you and I'm free. Now I realize that nudge behind me was you all along. Finally I recognize you God, but I've never really liked that name. There seem to be so many conflicting ideas of what you are, too much room for getting it wrong. And that is the funny part, all those ideas are right, because how you show up for me is mine. And how you show up for him is his. And my filter of love is purple, his is yellow. We are looking at, feeling the same love, but it looks purple from here. Yellow from there. I like yellow too. I can feel yellow. I can at least be open to yellow because what I know is that we are all looking at the same thing, love.

So my story today begins with an awakening, to love and God on the plane and what could matter more? My story will continue when in the arms of the others also arriving here today, we lift each other up in healing love. Red, yellow, purple, orange, green, blue…and we all meld together into one amazing, magnetic rainbow, that yes, is magical. No doubt this colorful force has powers, super powers, that some can't fathom. It's true and real, my purple self has felt it so many times now there is no room left for doubt. And to live in a space without doubt dragging you down, well, that is freedom. Quiet, powerful, colorful, super-powered freedom, that once felt, never dies.

If for a moment you feel weighed down with doubt, meaning you have a brief forgetting, and you go unconscious to love, no worries. That freedom you know will immediately shine through the cracks of your doubt and blast the darkness. You won't lose your freedom. You never lost it in the first place…you were looking for purple. And maybe it was yellow that day."

Leaning over, I looked around at the sleeping passengers and thought, *oh my gosh, what was that?* I tucked the journal away and closed my eyes, not thinking much more of it until I arrived at the class the next morning.

At the airport, I met my blind date for the week: a fellow healer I planned to share a room with at the class. We hugged, and headed for the rental car spot, started talking about our lives and pretty much didn't stop talking until we were forced to shut up in class the next day. Ronda, a soul-sister, plopped into my crazy, divinely-orchestrated life that week, and I thought, *okay, this isn't random.* Up until and since that time, I never share rooms at events, always craving the solitude of a week away to rest and recharge from my normal mom/wife life. Call it divine intervention, serendipity, magic, or whatever; I don't care. I knew I was being surrounded with a magical sort of energy that week, and the Universe would prove it for me the next day.

When I arrived at the class, everything in me wanted to read the words I'd written on the plane. *You need to read it,* a voice kept telling me. *This was meant to share. It's not just for you,* the voice kept on me. I was so nervous. My heart pounded so hard that I looked down, convinced I was lurching slightly with each beat. I couldn't get myself to raise my hand (as many all around me were already doing, with questions and comments). I was too scared; after all, why would anyone want to hear what I had to say?

During our first break, I found courage somewhere in my small body.

"Can I read something I wrote?" I asked our instructor, my stomach churning. The simple act of speaking up and asking to do something I wanted to do, to read something I had written, felt torturous inside and usually paralyzed me. Today, something was different. I acted despite the way my body felt.

The 220 students returned from the break, and John walked up on stage. "Someone wanted to read something?" he said. I quickly put my hand up and stood with my journal before the usual me could back down. With an alien voice, I read my piece from beginning to end, without missing a step, a word or a breath. I wasn't asked to speak up (as others had been), and as I dared to glance up from the page between sentences, I was met with hundreds of smiling faces. They weren't bored. They weren't annoyed. They weren't giving me any kind of weird looks. They were listening. I felt worthy.

As I read the words, my whole body shook, but my voice did not waver. The students closest to me could see the book shaking in my hands, but the love they surrounded me with held me up and kept me reading like one of those New York City poetry slammers. To this day, I'm still not sure how I was able to write and read that piece, but it felt like the real me was born in that moment. Like I had a direct line to Source through my words. That all I had to do was get out of the way and let it flow.

The best part of the moment was when I uttered the last word and sat down, a little too fast…and the entire room erupted in applause. The sound gave me goosebumps. I sat in that seat and continued to shake for a few minutes. My chest ached. My heart pounded. My hands quivered, slowly returning the notebook back to its pocket in my purse.

"Thank you for sharing your poem," one woman said at the next break. I heard those words, looked into her eyes, and mine must have given my whole life of unworthiness away. *My poem?* I thought. *They think it was a poem.* I took a deep breath, stood there in the dim light of the ball-room with my eyes watering, and let myself become a poet. In the three months afterward, forty-eight poems came. Moving through fear had become my tool to accessing my soul. I had a taste of what it felt like to kick fear in the ass… and I wasn't letting go.

I left that room different than when I'd entered. The moment of moving through the feeling of fear, expressing myself out loud despite it, and then being fully and unconditionally accepted for the real me was a healing moment. Nobody laid hands on me. Nobody gave me a pill or tried to fix anything. Acting despite my fear was the answer.

That moment redefined healing for me and changed my life. That day, the brave healer, writer and poet was born. That day, shame had no place in my soul. That day, the real me was celebrated.

Ever since then, when the familiar feeling of heart-thumping, stomach-churning fear rumbles around inside me, I wake up a little more. I think about what it is I'm about to do, say, create, or try, because when I feel that certain way, I know it matters. The feeling of fear has become a steadfast compass, an internal GPS system for my soul. I pay close attention now. When fear shows up, I expect a miracle.

Big Brave Question: What if, instead of making you smaller, the feeling of fear could crack you open? What if fear was the way to your dreams?

Recently, I sat in a new spot I created for my writing—a bar table in front of my sliding glass door that looks out into my backyard at a really cool, old Dogwood tree—when a Facebook message popped up.

"I was there the day you read that poem to our class," the note said. "That was an amazing day!"

I've received several notes like that since my awakening, almost four years ago now. Little gifts from the Universe to remind me: Your fear is boring. Do bigger things.

11
Changing the World

When I started to write more and get published, my soul lit up. Hours would fly by as I sat clicking away on my keyboard. This thing I loved so much was filling me up, and all I wanted to do was write and inspire people.

Meanwhile, during my regular job with clients, I found myself looking up at the clock several times an hour. What was happening to me? I always boasted about loving my job. There wasn't anything about my career as a healer I regretted. But when I sat to express myself and began sharing my voice with others, I started feeling new, different and intensely passionate feelings about it. I knew what I was born to do.

I sat in the car talking to my mom on the phone one day, and she asked me how my writing workshop was coming along. Before I could get all the words out, I burst into tears. "I think this's what I was born to do, Mom."

Since that day in the car, my passion and purpose have grown and my courage has expanded with them. I consider the obstacles redirects and the mistakes I make, stepping stones. Everything I do, with this fiercely-alive purpose and passion, is feeding my soul. These are the very gifts I'm meant to share. The knowing is palpable. The acknowledgement is consistent.

What are your gifts?

Not sure? How about an exercise to help you find out?

Warrior Exercise: It's About How You Feel

Start by connecting with your body and breath as in previous exercises. Clear your mind and settle down deep into your body, being curious about whatever you notice. Practice releasing, softening and letting go with each exhale.

Pick up your pen, notebook and timer. Set your timer for five minutes and fill in the blank: What I really desire is _____.

Big Brave Question: What does warrior joy feel like?

This was my favorite chapter to write; I love helping others uncover the secret to living a more joyful life than you ever thought possible. What's your bliss? Have you had a taste of bliss yet? Hint: What do you love? What lights you up? What do you love to do so much that you lose track of time?

When I was asked these big questions, my answer was immediate and clear. Write! I've spent hours and days in a blissful state, writing—my heart's desires, the secrets to life, my insights and aha's, my experiences and reflections—in poems, essays, articles, blogs and books. But until someone asked me the question and related it to a possible change in my life, I was somewhat oblivious to the possibilities.

It was easy to tell people what I loved to do. Yet there was an old belief still in the way: "You're not good enough to make a living from your hobby." My desires functioned as sacred trail markers, lighting the path in front of me. But I didn't see them at first. I was too afraid to make the shift, to take the risk of pursuing my dreams.

It's probably right in front of you—you just have to get used to feeling it. So, what do you love? Sometimes we have to give ourselves permission to feel the good. We're so good, so practiced, at suffering, but we stifle ourselves when it comes to joy. Why? We know by now that the conditioned thoughts and beliefs that we'll be punished for speaking up, talking back or being too loud are old news. So, what's the new us, the new you, going to do about those burning desires now?

I mentioned a book by Gay Hendricks earlier called *The Big Leap.* He talks about something interesting and important: "The Upper Limit

Problem." He says we have a low tolerance for feeling joy and bliss, and every time we do something we count as a win in this category, we do something to sabotage it...and go right back into our comfort zone, which is feeling "meh."

Why do we do this? I don't know; he explains it some in the book, but I'm more about recognizing when something resonates and taking action, with awareness, to do something different. So that's what I suggest you do, too. When do you retreat to your comfort zone? Why do you do it?

Use the powerful tool of awareness to find where you're messing things up, just when they're getting good, and stop that! Choose another way to believe or act! Aren't you fed up with your old patterns? Aren't you ready for the adventure? I thought so.

I call this "flipping the switch." And it leads us to some powerful exercises.

Warrior Exercise: Flipping the Switch

Let's do a quick writing exercise. Get your notebook, pen and timer and set it for five minutes. This time I want you to write as fast as you can! Speed write and fill in the blank: I am grateful for_____. No rules, just write without stopping for five minutes.

Awesome. You just wrote out five minutes' worth of things you can flip your switch to when you're feeling sad, angry, depressed or judgmental. What do I mean by flipping the switch? When I have moments of fear, doubt, shame or uncertainty, I'm able to immediately use my awareness to observe those thoughts, recognize my fear voice or inner critic message, and use those feelings as an opportunity.

From that place of insight, the next—and most important—step is to change the negative thought to a positive one. And I don't mean by avoiding or stuffing your feelings. If you flip the switch before you feel the feeling, you'll be forced to feel that feeling again somewhere down the line. Feel fully first. Then release and let it go completely. Use "flipping the switch" to find something about the situation to feel grateful about. Like how I flipped the situation of growing up with my dad from anger and judgement to gratitude that it led me on this journey of bliss. Ask yourself: what better, more healthy way can I choose to think, believe and act toward this? Looking for the positive in negative circumstances helps to flip your mindset to one of gratitude and joy.

The Law of Attraction states that like attracts like. If I want to feel grateful, loving, inspired, joyful and magical, I need to cultivate those feelings first. They won't come if I'm in a mindset of worry, doubt, or fear. The beauty is that with the powerful tool of awareness you've been practicing throughout this book, you have the choice about how to think, believe and act. We can flip the switch any time we want to; it's all a matter of awareness.

When we flip the switch to the magic, we attract more magic. We can't flip it if we don't know it needs to be flipped, though. Awareness is the key to opening the door of opportunity. I'm talking about a fierce awareness. You must learn to watch your thoughts like a hawk. Understanding that our default mindset can be negative, we have to notice it often so we can change the pattern.

Now that we are acute observers of what's going on in that mind of ours, we get to decide what we want to flip the switch to. Gratitude's always my go-to, but I also use love, magic, miracles, joy and bliss. In fact, the more you focus on these positive feelings, the more you will attract situations that have you feeling more of them.

Now we're going to create another list to use when you're ready to flip your switch.

Warrior Exercise: Love Energy

Let's do one more writing exercise. Set your timer for five minutes and fill in the blank: I love_____. No rules, just write as fast as you can for five minutes without stopping.

After playing with gratitude lists and the amazing energy of gratitude, I started to dig a little further and think about what I really love. I'm not talking about kinda love. I'm talking about stuff that really turns me on, lights my fire and gets me excited enough to move me. When you're in touch with these feelings and desires, you have powerful fuel.

When what we love is our daily focus, more of what we love shows up. That's the Law of Attraction in a nutshell: it's all an energy exchange. Everything is energy. Every single thought and emotion has a vibration of energy. Some of those thoughts are lower in vibration (think negativity, fear, worry, doubt, etc.) and some are a higher vibration (think love, bliss, joy, gratitude, passion, etc.). When we start to develop the powerful practice of using our awareness to flip the switch, it really behooves us to flip it to the higher vibration thoughts. We have to get ourselves vibrating higher, and we vibrate higher when we choose love. Not just thinking about the word, but feeling the sensation it creates within us.

So, what do you love? What really turns you on? What lights your fire? What do you truly desire? What gets you really excited? Give yourself permission to dive into these feelings often. It's who you are at your core. Uncover that light.

Do you hear your inner critic when you shift your thoughts to the positive? What does she say? Notice what happens when you're flipping the switch. Is there any resistance? Any lingering voices? Notice any sensations? You're using awareness to notice what's happening, and then you can decide to direct your focus to a feeling of love, or joy, or happiness, just like when you bring your attention back to the breath. It's that easy.

The questions about what you love are all excellent writing prompts, so when you need a boost, come back to them and spend a few minutes in that kind of energy, by writing more things that light you up. The more often you focus on love, the more you will attract that energy to your life.

Warrior Exercise: Visualizing Love

I'm going to talk you through a wonderful body awareness exercise that'll help bring your attention inward a little bit differently. We're going to combine awareness with visualization. Put your notebook aside and get comfortable. Take a few deep breaths. Close your eyes and begin by sinking down deep into your chair or mattress. Clear your mind and let go. Let all the tension in your body melt away into the earth. Take another couple deep breaths and let go even deeper. Let the surface you're sitting or lying on take all the weight of your body and make space inside by relaxing, unclenching and softening from head to toe.

Begin to imagine a beautiful luminescent light in the center of your chest. As you begin to feel it, notice where it is. What does it look like? What color is it? How big is it? Does it have a temperature? Breathe deeply into your belly as you notice and observe the beautiful luminescent light inside of you. With the next few breaths, allow that light to grow and fill your torso. And then allow it to expand into your arms. Feel it as it travels all the way to your fingertips. Now allow it to expand through the pelvis and down the legs. Feel it as it travels all the way to the toes. Let it expand upward through your neck and into your head. Feel this beautiful luminescent light as it fills your entire body with energy and love.

Now, let the light get even bigger than the borders of your body. Feel it as it expands beyond your skin, out into the room. How does this feel? Breathe deeply as you release and relax, allowing this beautiful light to fill every cell and then out beyond your body to the world around you. Notice, allow the flow and let go.

Allow this beautiful light to fill you down to your soul and then up and out to the stars.

Let yourself float in the feeling of being held by this loving, nurturing light.

Let your breathing soften and quiet down. Take a deep belly breath as you bring your awareness back into your body and the room around you. Slowly open your eyes when you are ready.

Take a moment to move slowly and stretch your limbs before you grab your notebook and pen. Notice the feelings in your body. Be curious and open to any messages your inner warrior is communicating.

Set your timer for five minutes and write about this: What do you love to do so much that you lose track of time? Write like you're talking to your

BFF. Let them feel, see, taste, hear and smell what you're talking about. Speaking of BFF's, sharing your gifts requires a warrior community.

Now that you're a warrior, decide who you're going to recruit to join you on this sacred mission. This's important. The people we invite to our sandbox will affect our energy, emotions and actions. Who do you want in your soul sandbox with you?

"I don't have a choice," you may say. "The people I live with or spend most of my time with don't get it." I understand completely, but the new level of awareness you're practicing will force you to do one of two things: change your environment, or aim to educate.

You may need to redistribute the time you spend with negative people. You may need to speak up and voice your needs. You may need to tell others what you're doing and who you aim to be, especially those who've known you the longest.

I've always been lucky to have a few people in my life who stick by me, no matter what crazy "phase" I'm going through. It never matters what new idea or project I'm working on, they support me and love me through it. And I've always had a few people in my life who question everything and make me doubt myself. Their support seems conditional, judgmental and opinionated.

Both kinds of people are a gift.

I see value in both kinds of people because if it weren't for the second group of naysayers, I wouldn't know what I don't want. The second group has given me laser clarity. The second group has allowed me to practice being myself no matter who I'm with or where I am. But I don't choose to fill my life with the second group now.

Choose Who Gets to Share Your Precious Time

I'm pacing the kitchen, listening to the phone ring.

"Hello?" The sound of Shelly's voice makes me smile.

"OMG, Shell, I have to share something with you! Remember that gig I applied for, you know, with the billionaire? I got it!" I blurted out.

"Oh my God, that's great!" The tone in her voice moves up about thirty decibels; exactly where it should be, exactly the level of celebration mode my news deserves. She does this instantaneously and genuinely.

I'm pickier about who I let into my little world now, about the people with whom I spend my precious time and surround myself, those I count on to support my dreams. With awareness, I get to choose my posse. That aware choice makes a difference when it comes to my success. It makes a difference for my mindset. The people I count on hold me accountable to my big dreams.

"Please, guys, don't let me back down on this." I'm typing the email, feeling brave because it's probably the hundredth time they've received an email from me asking for help. "This really matters to me," I continue writing. "When I start to tell you I'm not good enough, I need you to tell me I am, okay?" Basically, I'm asking them to not let me quit and fall into believing my inner critic. We all need help with this.

During my marriage, my self-worth as a healer was challenged on a daily basis. The man I married is a hard-working, traditional, "life should be difficult," kind of guy. He's dotting every "i" and crossing every "t" in the perfect employee and achievement categories. It was hard for him to understand the warrior hippie healer in me. Even harder for him to not judge my dream to heal the world with my writing as me being in fantasyland.

"You aren't planning on writing another one, are you?" My (now ex) husband commented one day about my poetry journal. "I thought your first real book was good, I told you that. But this, this doesn't seem viable to me."

In that moment, I realized I was afraid to tell him about the divine intervention on the plane. Afraid to let him in on the magic of my poetry. Afraid to let him know that writing has become my bliss, that hours pass by without me realizing it. Because of my fear, I never allowed him to come on my journey.

When he made that comment, I already had a publishing date for my second journal. The horrible, sinking feeling inside of me left me quiet, small and speechless. My inner three-year-old showed up full force. I kept getting the message that being myself in my marriage wasn't going to be easy or okay.

I fought every single day for a long time to take my marriage on as the biggest opportunity I had to express my true self, and to overcome my fear of communicating my dreams. I've had to realize if it weren't for my ex, I may have never tackled my biggest battles and gone after a more authentic kind of healing and love. There're gifts in our most difficult relationships. I had to do the radical forgiveness thing here, too.

Your posse should overpower everyone else from a support perspective, but that support doesn't have to come from just one person or one group. If you're putting too many of your "warrior community" eggs in one basket, you'll end up completely disappointed. It's okay to have friends that help you drive the kids to camp and friends who can talk Mercury Retrograde. Other people in your life might support other needs, like lover, best friend, and confidant.

The biggest mistakes we make with our relationships are not having enough diversity, believing we should do everything on our own, or counting on one person for everything. I have certain friends who inspire me to paint and others who make me a better writer. Some help me raise my kids, and others help me keep my healing skills up to par.

There's one deal-breaker here and it's toxicity. When toxic people show up, we're required to call on all the tools of awareness we've practiced so far: recognizing the inner critic, feeling the negative sensations in our body, listening to intuition, and being brave. People who're a consistent drain of your positive energy, or are mentally or physically abusive, or are toxic, should be deal-breakers as far as admittance to your inner circle. Get yourself out of that situation. You may not be able to remove those people from your life entirely (in the case of family or colleagues), but being in proximity to them doesn't mean you have to subject yourself to their negativity. When their toxic sides rear their ugly heads, find a way to change the subject or simply excuse yourself and walk away.

I've had to differentiate other peoples' toxicity with my own shit being triggered. Because I've healed much of myself and can now accept people for where they are in their own healing process, I'm often able to feel where they're at. Sometimes when I shine my light at them they're aware enough to feel it and present enough to do that dance with me. Sometimes I can shine until the sun goes down and it never makes a difference…the person is seeing the world through their negative filter, their "right" and "perfect" filter, and nothing I can do will change it.

If I realize that it's my own trigger that sets me off, lately I've been practicing giving myself permission to be vulnerable and let others know how I feel. I can't tell you it feels any better or lighter than it ever did before, but I can tell you the faster I go there, the easier and softer things get. The quicker I can speak up about my feelings, the quicker things are resolved. I don't have to be right all the time; in fact, nowadays I'd rather just hurry up and be wrong, let the other person win, and then make a decision if I want to spend more time with them.

In every instance, I have to decide if a person is toxic and not good for me, or if a communication challenge is worth the effort. If I sense the person can have a rational, aware discussion, and worst case scenario, agree to disagree, then game's on. If not, I quickly let them win, then excuse myself from the interaction. It's not worth my time if someone doesn't enjoy the big questions, understand the awareness thing, or respect me enough to listen.

I got a huge shot of "you better walk your walk" just now, and the best thing about writing my truth down on paper for the world to read is that it holds me accountable. One thing people are afraid of is speaking about what they believe, maybe because as soon as it's out there, you'll be held to it by your readers. This's a good thing! You can always change your mind, but owning your shit, sharing your healing and expressing your aware thoughts inspires you to do and be better.

"Do the best you can until you know better. Then when you know better, do better." — Maya Angelou

If you want something, say it out loud. Find someone you can have "that" kind of conversation with and tell them. Dream big, and don't keep it to yourself. If you want something to feel real, the best way to make that happen is to tell someone, get accountable and take action. Schedule that action on your calendar, just like your work appointments. It has to matter that much!

Build Your Warrior Community

A warrior community is a group of like-minded souls who keep each other brave and in action. There's a healthy version of competition mixed with collaboration and support. It's worth the time and effort to craft this group carefully. To be okay with saying no, and to trust your intuition. It doesn't serve you to feel anything but blissed out when it comes to the people who help you on your healing journey.

When you figure out what you love doing so much that you lose track of time, the next step to bliss is immersing yourself in a circle that'll help you do more of your thing. There's an intensely powerful energy in collaboration. There's a tight, lacking, negative energy in competition. Part of the warrior awareness you have cultivated will serve you as you build your circle and make connections.

In building my warrior community, I've also sought out several teachers and mentors. Everyone in my life's a teacher of some sort, but I'm talking about the people who've been where I want to be and can offer their wisdom and resources to help me get there too. The most powerful influencers are those who are doing what you want to do. These people are not competition. They are teachers. The good ones are, anyway.

Be brave, reach out, ask, take the risk, set up the date, hire the coach. The action you take will expand automatically because when you show the Universe you mean business, it will organize on your behalf.

I've found people in many different ways. Some showed up in my Tae Kwon Do class, some on Facebook, some next door, and some at stores

I frequent. Keep your mind and heart open. It's never too late to make a best friend.

Warrior Exercise: My Circle

This one is solely a writing exercise. Grab your notebook, pen and timer and set the timer for five minutes. Imagine yourself being coached by the ultimate, wildly successful, totally heart-centered and supportive community. I want you to describe the who, how, when and why of this person or people. Every detail. Remember, no rules, just write without stopping for five minutes.

Big Brave Question: Who is already doing what you want to do?

Warrior Homework: Find a way to contact that person and interact.

Warrior action is how everything's going to happen, no matter what it is you want. Without action, your hopes and dreams are just thoughts in your head.

If I left this part of the book out, you might as well throw it all away: it's that important. Action is to success like breathing is to survival...your dreams will die without it.

You started this book with the action of practicing awareness, in all of its forms. You continued taking action by being brave and finding ways to express yourself inside of that awareness. When it came time to heal your shit, you continued to act by seeking out ways to peel off the layers and get to your soul. And through the action of staying awake and finding your bliss, you started feeling the purpose and mission of your life.

Or you just read this whole book and haven't taken any action at all!

I hope not, because the trick to getting anything you want lies in taking action, small or big, on a daily basis.

I've become known as "The No Grace Period" goddess. I don't wait when something feels right. I've also been judged as irresponsible and impulsive for the same thing. One thing I know is this method works, no matter what names doubters want to call me. I get closer and closer to the things I desire by taking lots of action and by not letting mistakes or failures derail me for long. I use those obstacles as stepping stones to the me I want to be.

Fear—most often of failure, making mistakes, or being wrong—gets in the way of taking action. Until the day I stood up in the ballroom of 220 people and read my poem, I was never able to raise my hand, even for a simple question. I was terrified of being "out there" and of criticism. I wasn't willing to risk feeling humiliated. The fear was so palpable and so paralyzing that I never took any risks and was stuck staying small and feeling tight. And then feeling resentful and disappointed in myself.

Those feelings held true in the classroom and in my life overall. It was the same kind of fear everywhere I went, with everyone I met. *They'll think I'm stupid,* ran through my head often. *He'll be so pissed,* was another frequent occupier of space in my mind. *He will leave you,* usually followed. So instead of speaking up and expressing myself, I stayed quiet, small, and powerless, letting the events and people in my life run it for me.

UGH.

The action you'll now take, as a warrior, will have to do with the things you love, the magic you want to do in the world, the person you strive to be, the desires that light your fire. Your soul's calling. This kind of action is the magic sauce that turns those dreams into reality.

Here's the best part: the magic's happening right in the middle of every mistake or failure you make. Those things are just little stepping stones for you too, and each one of them has an arrow pointing toward your dreams. Might as well step faster.

The mistakes we're afraid to make mark the path to our bliss. Do you get this?

Action is to success like breathing is to survival. You are keeping your dreams alive by moving toward them, action step by action step, mistake by mistake, victory by victory. It doesn't really matter how that stepping stone shows up, it's still moving you forward. Mistakes that feel like you're back-peddling are actually just redirecting you.

The biggest problem with those mistakes, failures and wrong steps is that we're giving them meaning and attention. The meaning we give an event can be the difference between it causing paralyzing depression and it being a mere blip on our journey. Begin to see the failures as just another step forward. And keep stepping. The more mistakes you make, the faster you'll arrive.

"When we stop opposing reality, action becomes simple, fluid, kind and fearless." — Byron Katie

When I figured this out, I became a crazy machine of action, intermixed with aware stillness. My action became purposeful, so it was efficient. I had more time to get still and contemplate my next move. Sitting around and worrying, stressing or obsessing about saying or doing something that isn't quite what I want or expect? That's a waste of precious time, and I have way too much to do to waste more time.

Warrior action is consistent, purposeful, aware, thoughtful and generous. I try to remember gratitude and love in all my actions, because that's the power that attracts more awesomeness to my endeavors. Warrior action is a creative expression of you! If actions speak a thousand words, then warrior action basically shows the world who you are and who you aim to be. It's one of the windows to your soul.

What do you want? That thing you love to do—tell me about it. What do you need to do to make sure more of that happens every day? Make a list of action steps leaning in the direction of that thing; it doesn't matter how big or small they are. Making the list is a start.

What matters to you? When you think about prioritizing your time, what're the things that matter the most in your life? Do more of those. How will you make sure that what really matters is what you're spending your time taking action on? What needs to occur to make that happen?

Remember, I get high on big questions. I swim in them day and night. When I get off track, I remember to ask myself big questions, and I'm soon back in the game. If I fall asleep and lock myself up in that box in my head, I don't stay there too long. I know my defaults, my fears, my Martha...so when I recognize one of those, I choose another way to think and unlock that box. It's totally up to me. And in your life, it's up to you!

Every action you take, when bathed in loving warrior awareness, is an action for your bliss, even when the outcome isn't what you expected. I've learned to trust what is. I sometimes think something didn't work out, or that something is bad, or wrong, or sad, or tragic, until I see the meaning in it...sometimes years later. I've learned not to believe everything I think, trust what's happening is not random, and be curious instead of upset. *Hmm, that's interesting!* Is what I say to myself when something weird/bad/horrible/unexpected/totally off the wall happens. Then I go right back to focusing on what feels good. (In other words, I flip the switch.)

Living in wonder and curiosity helps my stress levels, too. Curiosity takes the edge off disappointment most days. Choose to be curious rather than upset. And if you come up against resistance here, guess what? You might have discovered more shit to heal.

Several years ago, I took a personal growth course called The Landmark Forum. At our break, we had specific homework: to make a call to a person about whom we'd had an aha moment during the morning session. This wasn't easy homework. This was about being seriously vulnerable and calling to tell the person that you had been wrong or stubborn and that you wanted to move forward in the relationship differently. It was about rescinding blame and apologizing...it was about giving up being right. I called my dad that day.

"Hey Dad. I'm here at this class this weekend, and we were asked to do some homework. I wanted you to know that I think I've spent my whole life blaming you for everything. I'm realizing I've been stuck in that old story, and I'm sorry." I shook as I spoke. I could feel everything in me resisting the vulnerability.

From that day forward, my ability to communicate with my dad changed. It's not perfect, and I have some more healing to do, but it was a huge start. That phone call, that little bit of action, changed everything.

Big Brave Question: What phone call do you need to make?

One last thing about this. You may find yourself developing a lower tolerance for bullshit, small talk, gossip or anything else that isn't a byproduct of the new awareness you've cultivated or doesn't align with your bigger dreams and purpose. Be ready for some of the people in your life to fall away. Every action you take will have consequences, and sometimes what serves you might rub someone else the wrong way. It's okay to stand for yourself, and it's okay to let go of whatever doesn't serve you anymore.

Warrior Magic

Dreams, magic, miracles, fairy dust, unicorns and rainbows…that's what my days are made of, even if people think I live in a fantasy world. Am I crazy? Maybe. But it beats living 24/7 in fear, doubt, negativity, shame and difficulty. Life's hard, if you think it is. Or you can practice your magic, your special blend of positive, on-purpose bad-assery. Sprinkle your sparkle wherever you go and see who follows the trail. It's more fun this way.

I'm tired of being told what the realities of life are. I recognize people are looking through their own filter and I can appreciate and accept them where they are, but I don't have to agree or go along with it. I refuse to be a zombie. I refuse to stress just because I'm supposed to. I refuse to be so serious about life.

One night before my divorce, I sat on the patio with my husband and felt brave, so I began telling him about this book.

"I have this new book idea," I said.
"Oh yeah? What is it?" He replied.

"It's a book about healing."

"What does your family think about that?" He asked, recalling the rough response I had to the memoir I wrote about my childhood.

"It's not that book," I said. "This one's about helping people heal. I'm excited." He wasn't. He wanted to know what I was writing and how much time I was taking out of my regular job to write.

"What if it's a bestseller?" I said, fighting for my dream.

"You're in a fantasy world," he said. For a moment, I contemplated the world in my head, the dreams I had, and the goals I had for my writing… with huge doubt. Then I had to practice what I preach and let the tightness in my chest dissolve with the next exhale. I had to find a place inside I believed in, no matter how big the fantasy.

"It might seem like a big goal, but this's important to me, and I know I can do it." I finished and walked away. That interaction would be the beginning of the clarity I needed to make a huge change and ask for a divorce. It was when I realized that the most important person in my life was not going to support me in my big dreams.

You're holding the proof of my bravery in your hands. If I hadn't written this book, hadn't taken consistent action and practiced my magic, I would have quit and stayed resigned to my small life. What if I had believed him?

I do things differently than a lot of other people. Many can't tolerate my quick action and warrior style. I rub people the wrong way sometimes. I'm too much. "It takes stamina to roll with you," my coach said. "And that's okay. You don't need to dull down who you are for the world."

I don't agree with traditional avenues of living, working or parenting. I don't like playing by rules. I like making my own. I question everything and don't believe in a "right" way in life or business. I believe I can redefine almost anything that doesn't serve my purpose or the purpose of healing the world.

I believe in miracles and magic. Warrior magic is the way you look at the world around you. It's how you perceive things. It's an energy of pure spirit. It's knowing you're here with a purpose. When you are still and grounded in that spirit, things show up, messages are given, what you need manifests, people call, offers are made, your thoughts become things. Warrior magic is a combination of the Law of Attraction and the mystical world. It's in my amethyst crystal and the hawk that flies overhead. It's in that thing I hear on the radio at just the right moment and the repeating numbers on my clock.

Magic exists if you believe it does. Let's do a magical exercise now.

Warrior Exercise: Discover Your Magic

Let's do a short exercise to ground and center in the power of our own magic. Take a seat, relax and breathe deeply. Follow the breath three or four times, with each exhale softening more into your body. Bring your energy down into your core and let go all the way to your toes. Feel that core energy come up and connect with your heart, soften and feel it all the way to the top of your head and out to your fingertips. Breathe, relax, soften and let go. Give yourself permission to feel. What are the sensations you notice? Breathe three or four more deep breaths and continue to soften around any sensations you notice. With each breath you are both more centered and still, and more light and free at the same time. Take one more deep breath as you contemplate the questions below. Live inside of the questions themselves.

What magic shows up in your life? What are the ways the Universe talks to you? Do you see the magic in the sunrise? What about in the creatures that you share the earth with? How about the serendipitous moments? Do you allow yourself to feel pure joy? What are your limits?

Grab your notebook, pen and timer. Set your timer for five minutes and write on this: When I see and feel the magic it shows up like this _____.

Big Brave Question: Do you believe in magic?

Warrior Attitude

You're not who you say you are, you are what you do.

When positivity marries indomitable spirit, the warrior attitude is born. It takes a warrior to live her life awake in each moment, rather than asleep and reacting to everything that happens. This attitude must be repeated tirelessly, no matter the internal or external resistance.

This chapter is about repeating the behavior you want and need to repeat in order to create the life you desire. Repetition—when it creates a discipline that includes a warrior attitude and serves your dreams and desires—is what allows you to manifest what you want. My son has a poster on his bedroom wall that says, "Attitude determines your altitude in life." If you want to be lifted higher, you need to set your attitude first.

How do you think, believe and act every day? Is it in alignment with what you say you want? It pays to be critical here. Investigate your behavior. Watch it. Be curious. Figure out where you're on target and where you're not. Pay attention to where you are and put your intention into that. Repeat often.

Go back to chapter one if you need to get another boost of the main skill I'm talking about. A warrior attitude is born from awareness. You choose to think the right thoughts and believe certain things and take particular action. You create your life. A warrior attitude is essential.

Please don't *try* to have one. Just have one. Trying to do something is an excuse for not doing it. "I'm trying" and "I'll try" are wimpy. Just go for it. It will either work out or not, and if it doesn't, remember: it's a stepping stone.

Take on the attitude that you already have what you want. "Fake it?" You ask. Sure, if that's what it takes. When you expect things, the Universe has a way of making it so. That's an attitude. It's intense…but you're a warrior. Your expectations and feelings drive your manifestations.

Being on-purpose is the laser-focused attitude you'll want to adopt if you care to change things. Stay awake in the moments of your day. Catch where you aren't being who you want to be. Journal about that a bit to clear out the debris. Then go back to your task in the next moment, and be brave.

The behaviors we repeat will turn into our default. You want your default behaviors to be badass! You don't want to skimp in this area. It's like tuning a radio: get the station in loud and clear and enjoy the music that happens as a result.

When you're afraid to be yourself, this all feels excruciating. I'm convinced introverts (the ones who claim to not be outgoing) are just afraid to express themselves. They're a bubbling burst of wild, creative expression in a very small cage. They're afraid to be themselves. It hurts in there. The bars of the cage exist in their own minds and are made of fear, doubt and shame.

I'm a recovering introvert. I'd describe it as painfully introverted. Please don't laugh. But if you do, I won't take it personally. In my 20's (when life was all about the social scene), going to parties and talking to people was excruciating. Why do I keep using that long word for painful? Because painful doesn't do the feeling justice. My insides felt so tight, constricted and painful, it was impossible to focus on anything but that agony... which made me a horrible person to talk to at a party. I couldn't get over myself, so I didn't know I should focus on others, ask them questions and be truly interested in them.

Today, things are hugely different. I enjoy connection, in all its forms. I'm comfortable in my own skin. I'm able to focus on and trust how I feel in the moment and let that lead me into interactions that feel nourishing. I look at meeting new people as exciting, and I'm always wondering what might happen next, rather than dreading putting myself out there.

How is it possible that one can go from being an introvert to being an extrovert? Because it's not something you're born into or stuck with for the rest of your life. I believe some aspects of introversion are fear and unworthiness.

I've just given you the key to your cage. Are you going to unlock it? Do you want to unlock it? Or are you safely in your comfort zone in there?

Through the process of waking up, being brave, healing my shit, staying awake, finding my bliss and making all of that the discipline of my life, I recovered. I now love talking to people. I don't fill my energy tanks by going to parties or PTA meetings (those actually drain me), but I truly enjoy being and expressing myself and learning about others now.

I enjoy making people laugh. I can be the center of attention (and not run out of the room) or create the focus for someone else to be that. I look and sound extroverted because I finally love myself and I'm not afraid of people not liking me. It's not my goal to have everyone not like me; I've just dropped the attachment to them liking me. I see the impossibility of that mindset. Do I still get triggered when someone's upset or disagrees with me? Yes. The difference is how I react and the speed with which I carry on.

Fear's the ticket here, again. Get over the fear, express yourself and find your worth, and you'll have a one-way ticket to healing your inner introvert and donning a warrior attitude that serves your huge dreams. Yes, huge! Why play small?

Warrior Life

Wake up. Be brave. Heal your shit. Do what you love. Repeat. The warrior life.

What does healing your way into a kick-ass life look like? Maybe not what you think. These lives of ours, even for warriors, contain sadness, difficulty and tragedy. A warrior life isn't about avoiding all these things, not experiencing them or hiding your emotions. It's about waking up with love, joy and passion in your heart despite them. It's about the attitude and practice of awareness you repeatedly choose inside of those things.

If it weren't for the sadness, difficulty, tragedy and trauma, we wouldn't understand the biggest love and joy. It's this contrast that gives us more opportunity. One doesn't have meaning without the other. Perspective's the friend of the warrior. So are gratitude and positivity. Add some determination and healthy amounts of persistence, and you have a warrior life.

In fact, try looking at the tragedies and traumas of your life as the exact things that allow you to do what you do, follow your dreams and help others heal (if that's your thing). You're qualified because of your experiences. It's the most difficult people in your life that become your teachers, if you look at it that way.

Be stubborn about your joy. Things that try to crush it are deal breakers. A warrior life is created with the awareness that life is made up of one fiercely alive choice after another. This awareness might be the only thing we have control over. The rest we have to surrender to.

If you find yourself trying to control anything outside of your own thoughts, know you'll lose. The warrior's battle is knowing that her own awareness, thoughts and responses to those thoughts are her only weapon. She has to learn everything else's out of her domain, and fighting or resisting any of it will cause pain.

I've already described the warrior life. I've given you tools for creating it. You know what to do. You get that it's important. You feel this mission from your toes to your soul. You are not alone. This matters. You live in the big questions. It's time to be brave. Share your gifts. Heal the world.

Warrior Exercise: My Blissed-Out Day

This is a writing exercise, so get your notebook and pen, but this time there is no time limit. This exercise was given to me by Torrie, the coach I mentioned earlier. Imagine you have no limitations (time, money, people, etc.). I want you to describe your perfect, blissed-out day, from the moment you wake up to the moment you fall asleep. Let us—your hypothetical readers, even if you decide to keep this to yourself—see, hear, smell, taste and feel every detail. Spare nothing. Let us feel what it's like to be in your bliss and how your life would play out in every amazing way. Take us on a journey of your dream.

Take a deep breath. Arrive fully into your body and soul. Relax, release and let go. No rules, just write. You are welcome to submit your perfect blissed-out day to me at bewarriorlove@gmail.com and I will choose a few to post (with your permission) as guest blogs on my site.

Big Brave Question: Now what?

The End

The end of this book is the beginning of your life. Run, don't walk, into your desires—those sacred trail markers. Don't let anything get in the way of who you want to be or what you want for your brave life. Make lighting the fire of inspiration your daily chore. Ignite your fire and shine that light so brightly, we can't help but stare.

I'm honored you chose to read these words. You're a brave healer! You're amazing. Your story matters!

With Warrior Love,

Laura

Warrior Questions

Here is a list of some big questions posed in the book, along with follow up questions. Use them in groups or discussions as talking points or on your own, as writing prompts. Live these questions and see how things start to shift.

What do you feel right now?

What do your emotions feel like?

What does your fear feel like?

Does that feeling come with an inner critic voice?

Give that voice a name…what is it?

What healing modalities have you tried?

How did they work for you?

If you could feel fear in your body and recognize it as a compass pointing you in the direction of your truth, what would your truth be?

How do you know your truth is the truth?

What shit do you need to heal?

What would you do if you weren't afraid?

What is one way you can stay awake to the stuff of your life?

What is another way?

What do you love to do so much that you lose track of time?

How often do you spend time doing what you love?

What really matters to you?

Who is already doing what you want to do?

How can you contact that person?

What collaborations are you dreaming up?

Do you believe in magic?

How does magic show up in your life?

Brave Healer Resources:

The Brave Healer Network - Join at www.BraveHealer.com

My free Facebook group: The Brave Healers Mastermind and Refuge

Laura's writing on Medium: www.medium.com

Business and Mindset Programs:
www.MarieForleo.com
www.LuckyBitch.com
www.WomenRockingBusiness.com

Breathwork:
www.experiencebreath.com

John F. Barnes Myofascial Release:
www.myofascialrelease.com

On Purpose Women Community:
www.GinnyRobertson.com

Personal Development and Coaching:
www.landmarkeducation.com
www.odettepeek.com

Tapping (Emotional Freedom Technique):
www.thetappingsolution.com

The Haven Writing Retreat:
www.LauraMunsonAuthor.com

Editing:
WriteAssociate.com

Blogging:
Jon Morrow, www.SmartBlogger.com

The Prosperous Writer's Mastermind:
www.HonoreeCorder.com

About the Author

Laura's a California girl who's lived on the East Coast raising her family for the last couple decades. After pursuing her physical therapy degree she started to feel the urge to write out loud and began by educating her clients about healing through her blog.

She always knew a book would come, and self-published her memoir, Living, Healing and Taekwondo, in 2012. Those stories give the reader a window into her life as a healer over a six-year period of time when she and her son trained for and earned their black belts together at Gentle East Tae Kwon Do.

Over a journey that includes working toward being a business owner, running three marathons, a twenty year marriage that ended in divorce, eleven years in the martial arts, two amazing teenagers, authoring countless inspirational blogs and four poetry journals, and starting her business as an inspirational speaker, she's learned the secrets of the Universe; awareness, gratitude, love and joy. She encourages us to go for the joy.

When she isn't writing something that turns you on you'll probably find her eating dark chocolate or Italian food, at a rave jumping until dawn, drag racing her Mustang, or finding a quiet spot at a winery with her notebook and pen to Feng Shui her soul.

You'll find Laura at BraveHealer.com and on her Facebook page @kickasswar-riorgoddess. Please also come join the Brave Healers Mastermind and Refuge, her free Facebook group for healers!

Other Books By
Laura Di Franco

Living, Healing and Taekwondo
Warrior Love, a Journal to Inspire Your Fiercely Alive Whole Self
Warrior Joy, a Journal to Inspire Your Fiercely Alive Whole Self
Warrior Soul, a Journal to Inspire Your Fiercely Alive Whole Self
Warrior Dreams, a Journal to Inspire Your Fiercely Alive Whole Self

Co-author projects:

What's in Your Web; Stories of Fascial Freedom, by Phil Tavolacci
Superwoman Myths, Break the Rules of Silence and Speak Up Your Truth, by Kristy Lea Tritz
365 Ways to Connect with Your Soul, by Jodi Chapman and Dan Teck

74977990R00099

Made in the USA
Middletown, DE
01 June 2018